D0403936

PERSONAL BUDGETING KIT

Sylvia S. Lim, CFP, CGA

Self-Counsel Press
(*a division of*)
International Self-Counsel Press Ltd.
USA   Canada

Printed in Canada

First edition: 2001; Reprinted 2002; 2003

Second edition: 2005; Reprinted 2006

Library and Archives Canada Cataloguing in Publication

Lim, Sylvia

    Personal budgeting kit / Sylvia S. Lim. — 2nd ed.

      First ed. published under title: Simply essential personal budgeting kit.

    ISBN 1-55180-654-1

    1. Budgets, Personal. I. Title.

HG179.L55 2005   332.024   C2005-904368-7

Material excerpted from *The Wordsmyth Educational Dictionary–Thesaurus* is used with permission.

Self-Counsel Press
(*a division of*)
International Self-Counsel Press Ltd.

1704 North State Street	1481 Charlotte Road
Bellingham, WA 98225	North Vancouver, BC V7J 1H1
USA	Canada

CONTENTS

1 **WHY BUDGET?**   1

    Financial Budgeting   2

    The Stress Factor   3

    The Fear Factor   4

    Defining Your Financial Goals   7

2 **THE BUDGET**   13

    Tracking Spending   13

        Daily spending   14

        Weekly spending   18

        Yearly spending   25

    Tracking Income   27

    Calculating Your Net Worth   31

3 **SPENDING MANAGEMENT**   39

    Analyzing and Revising Your Spending   39

    Changing Your Lifestyle   47

4	**DEBT MANAGEMENT**	**51**
	Paying Off Your Consumer and Credit Card Debts	51
	Paying Down Your Mortgage	54
	Your Credit Report	56
5	**SAVINGS MANAGEMENT**	**59**
	More to Savings than Savings Accounts	59
	Risk/Return	61
	Different Types of Investments	61
	Safety investments	62
	Income investments	62
	Growth investments	63
	Mutual funds	64
	Real estate investment	66
	The ABCs of Retirement Savings	68
6	**FINANCIAL PLANNING STRATEGIES**	**73**
	Tax Planning	73
	Estate Planning	74
7	**FREEDOM TO ENJOY LIVING**	**79**
	APPENDIX 1 —SAVINGS CHARTS	**81**
	Savings Chart 1	82
	Savings Chart 2	84
	Savings Chart 3	86
	Savings Chart 4	88
	APPENDIX 2 — TIPS ON SAVING MONEY	**91**
	GLOSSARY	**101**
	SAMPLES	
1	Financial Goals Worksheet	10

2   Daily Spending Worksheet   16

3   Weekly Spending Worksheet   20

4   Yearly Spending Worksheet   28

5   Income Worksheet   32

6   Net Worth Worksheet   36

7   Revised Spending Worksheet   42

TABLE

1   Mortgage Savings   54

1
WHY BUDGET?

Do you find yourself living from paycheck to paycheck? Do you worry about how you can make your next credit card payments? Even worse, do you feel helpless when you try to think about how you'll ever manage to retire at 65 (let alone "freedom 55") or do you try not to think about it at all? Most important, do you feel overwhelmed at the idea of coming up with a personal budgeting plan?

If the answer is yes to any or all of these questions, this kit is for you. It's a step-by-step guide to getting yourself back on track financially for the rest of your life. Along with all the necessary forms, it contains tips and information to help you create a workable personal budget. It simplifies the budgeting process, making it easy for you to create a solid, realistic plan. You will learn how to —

* set realistic financial goals,
* trim your spending painlessly,
* pay down your debt methodically,
* save and invest,
* develop a retirement savings strategy,
* make up an estate plan, and
* make over your lifestyle for a successful and stress-free future.

1

Financial Budgeting

You may feel you already know how to budget, or perhaps don't need to know, but your lifestyle can tell a different story. You may have trouble paying your bills, have no savings, be behind on your taxes, and generally not be able to make ends meet. Getting out of this rut takes some effort, but the rewards for doing so are high.

Simply put, developing a financial budget allows you to take charge of your finances. It means that you put into print how much you earn, how much you can spend, how much you will need to pay down your debts, and how much you can devote to savings. A financial budget is a blueprint that provides you with a direction to follow for the next few years. It allows you to take control of your spending and your financial life!

In addition to gaining greater control over your money, you can also employ financial budgeting to help you save for the big-ticket items you'd like to purchase. You can successfully use this kit to help you put aside money for —

* a car,
* your daughter's wedding,
* your children's college education,
* an extended vacation,
* a new kitchen in your home, and (of course)
* your own retirement.

Whatever your reason for wanting to be in charge of your money, the rules are the same. You must know what you want, where you stand financially, and how you will achieve your goals. With a little patience and some determination, you will find that budgeting becomes simply a new habit you've taken on and applied daily. In time, it will become second nature to you.

You don't necessarily need a lot of money to live a rich and full life. Many pleasurable things in life cost little or no money at all. But having a fulfilling, comfortable, and financially secure life requires some work on your part. You must commit yourself to good planning and work toward success a little at a time. A small dose of thriftiness and some good old common sense also help. Anyone can do it.

Commit yourself to following the steps in this book. You'll be glad you did. You may not become a millionaire overnight, but you will come away from the experience knowing and believing that you *can* be financially savvy. You'll be on your way to a more secure and comfortable future.

The Stress Factor

Perhaps you've woken up in the middle of the night with money concerns on your mind. Or perhaps on some nights you can't fall asleep at all. Maybe you find yourself edgy and irritable with those closest to you because you can't seem to get your mind off your financial troubles, and find that more and more, stress is negatively affecting your ability to enjoy your life.

Wordsmyth Educational Dictionary – Thesaurus defines stress as *a condition characterized by physical, mental, or emotional tension* (<www.wordsmyth.net>). *Webster's Collegiate Dictionary* defines it as *a physical, mental, or emotional strain or tension, a specific response by the body to a stimulus, as fear or pain, that disturbs or interferes with the normal physiological equilibrium.* As human beings, we often experience stress when we feel we are not in control of a situation. If stress accumulates, we may become physically sick, have insomnia, or experience depression-like symptoms. This emotional or intellectual tension may actually shorten life and certainly works to decrease its quality while we're living it. A recent World Health Organization (WHO) study found that 75 to 90 percent of all adult visits to primary care physicians in the industrialized world are for stress-related problems.

If you believe that by decreasing stress you can bring about a better quality of life for yourself and those around you, you will understand the importance of managing or eliminating situations that cause you needless anxiety. One of the major stressors in many people's lives is money — or, more precisely, lack of money-management skills. In fact, it is not knowing where you stand with your finances that causes the stress. For instance, you may —

* not know how much money is in your bank account when there are many bills to pay,
* not know how to go about paying all the bills that have piled up in the kitchen drawer,

* not know how long your current job (and paychecks) will last,
* worry about your inability to save because you don't know where your money really goes,
* worry about your inability to cover unexpected expenses or emergencies, and/or
* worry about not having enough money on which to retire.

So how can you deal with money-related stress effectively? Since it's almost impossible to eliminate money from your life without becoming poor, it's best that you learn how to manage it. First, confront the issue; then, learn to take charge of your own finances. Preparing a personal budget is a good start. You need to know exactly where you're at with your money — how much you own, how much you owe, how much is coming in, and how much is going out. The truth will set you free!

Personal budgeting is a useful and necessary exercise. Once you've taken a financial inventory, you can start managing your money more efficiently. You will be in control and can decide how to go about improving your situation. You can make informed decisions about your money.

If you keep spending more than you earn, constant debt is inevitable and bankruptcy is a very real possibility. You will continue to be stressed and remain unhappy with your life, no matter how much money you make. Take control of your life. If money management is a problem, make a point of dealing with it. Reduce your spending; reduce your stress. Take the plunge by continuing to read and work with this kit. It will be worth the effort, both in terms of your health and your pocketbook.

Money is a big worry for most people. But once you've gained control of your finances and learned to manage them effectively, you'll notice a reduction in your stress level, and that, in turn, will change your quality of life for the better.

The Fear Factor

Fear is an emotion humans experience when they perceive themselves to be in danger. It is an intense, unpleasant, and sometimes irrational feeling; one that can induce sensations of helplessness and paralysis, and in some cases, anger in those that experience it.

Some people find the thought of taking charge of their finances frightening. It is amazing how money can cause so much fear and anxiety in our society. Left unchecked, this fear can bring on not only insomnia and illnesses, but can also cause more damage to your happiness and life than you ever imagined.

Burying your head in the sand and ignoring your financial problems can have severe consequences. You may one day end up declaring bankruptcy and losing everything. A bankruptcy can leave you with a damaged credit rating and a ruined reputation, and can even destroy your relationships with the ones you love.

But you do have a choice. You can let your fear of money control you, or you can master it, and in doing so, do yourself one of the biggest favors ever.

Imagine this scenario. You've been having difficulty making ends meet for some time, and have been ignoring the bills that come in the mail because you don't have any money to pay them. The bills don't go away, though: they keep piling up. Some go overdue and start arriving with interest charges added to the amount you owe; some, such as the telephone and electricity bills, arrive accompanied by threats to terminate service. And other bills just keep coming. Many black marks begin to appear on your credit report, and you find it impossible to get loans or credit. If you allow your fear of confronting these bills to rule you, if you remain paralyzed, it won't be long before the bill collectors and bailiffs are knocking on your door, and maybe even on the door of your place of work. Because you can't pay, your creditors seize your assets. You now have no car, and maybe the TV is gone. The trouble and resulting stress affect your concentration, and you lose your job. Your family becomes pressured and stressed, and eventually breaks up. Your life spirals downward, and you lose all hope for the future. This may be a grim scenario, but it is a reality for many people. And all because they were frightened of dealing with their bills!

Now, look at another scenario. Let's say you decide *not* to ignore your unpaid bills. Instead, you start by setting limits on your spending. Next, you develop and follow a realistic financial budget. You now know how much money you can afford to devote to bill payments, so you contact your creditors to arrange a workable repayment plan with each of them, and maybe you even decide to consolidate your debts. You begin to simplify your lifestyle. After a period of time, you actually have your consumer debts — that is, your personal loans, household bills, and credit card balances — paid off. You begin saving for your future. Imagine, now, that it is three or four years later: you look back on your struggle for financial stability and feel a great sense of satisfaction in what you have accomplished. Your life looks bright, and you look forward to getting up every morning. You are physically and emotionally healthy, and have great hopes for the future.

That future — your future — is in your own hands. If you let fear consume you, it will make you inactive and control you. If you confront your fear, you are in control.

Train yourself to believe that you can take charge of your financial affairs. Have respect for money and for what it can do *for* you. Repeat to yourself every day that you are in control and can take action. Believe it. It's scary to realize that it's up to you, but you will feel better once you take the first step in realizing a more manageable financial future.

Defining Your Financial Goals

The first and most important step in the financial budgeting process is to decide what you want to gain from the task of mapping out a budget for yourself. You must decide on your financial goals; and more important, you must write these goals down. If you are serious about your goals, they are worth taking the time to ponder over and put down on paper. To make this exercise easier, a Financial Goals Worksheet is provided on the CD-ROM in both PDF and Word formats. Print the form and refer to a sample of the worksheet on page 10.

Listed below are examples of some common financial goals. You will notice that they include a dollar amount and a time period in which the goal can be reached. Each goal is realistic and measurable:

* Pay off credit card debt of $10,000 within four years.
* Pay off student loans of $7,000 within three years.
* Save $2,000 for a down payment on a first car within one year.
* Save $10,000 for a daughter's wedding within two years.
* Save $30,000 for children's college education within ten years.
* Save the equivalent of three months' wages ($9,000) for a family emergency fund in a year and a half.

Don't set yourself up for failure. Strive to make your goals as realistic as possible. It is fruitless to attempt to pay off your $10,000 credit card debt in one year if your take-home pay for that same year is only $25,000. You probably took a few years to accumulate such a debt. Allow yourself a few years to pay it off. The key to success in reaching your goals is a bit of patience and perseverance, but to begin with, the goals to which you commit yourself must be realistic. Take your time; you *will* make it. In the beginning, you may feel that it will take forever, but once you get into the habit of working toward your goals, they will become reality. In the meantime, this kit will give you advice and tips on making this endeavor as painless as possible.

> **tip:** A realistic financial goal must —
>
> * have a dollar amount,
> * have a time period for achievement,
> * be realistic, and
> * be measurable.

For this exercise, print the Financial Goals Worksheet from the CD-ROM included with this book. You will also need —

* a calculator (or preferably an adding machine with a tape feature);
* a pencil and an eraser for your calculations and writing; and
* a quiet, well-lit work space.

Complete the worksheet by following these steps:

1. Identify all your goals and write them down on the worksheet.

2. Prioritize these goals. Assign the number one to those that are most important to you, the number two to those that are somewhat important, the number three to those that are not so important, and the number four to those goals that fall into the category of "nice to have" but not urgent or necessary.

3. Record the dollar amount required to achieve each goal.

4. Calculate the monthly equivalent dollar amount for each goal.

5. Add up the monthly amounts of all goals to which you've assigned the number one. Record the total on the bottom of the page in the blank space beside "Total monthly amount."

You may find that you have several goals to which you've assigned a number-one priority. That simply means you're attaching the same level of importance to each of these goals. You'll probably end up working toward all your number-one-priority goals at the same time.

If you are part of a couple, both you and your partner should agree on and prioritize goals together. Open up the communications channel and talk freely about how each of you sees your financial future. Where do you want to be in three years' time, five years' time, and even ten years' time? Are your goals in sync? If not, negotiate and reach a compromise. It's important that in the end, you both are in full agreement about and completely aware of the family's financial goals. You must participate jointly in achieving them.

Determine the monthly amounts these goals will cost you by dividing each goal's dollar amount by the number of months you think it will take you to achieve. For example, if your goal is to pay off a $10,000 loan over four years (48 months), divide 10,000 by 48, which gives you a total of 208. You will need to set aside $208 each month to achieve that goal.

Finally, you (or you and your partner) should sign off on your goals, which will add another level of commitment to sticking with the budgeting habit. Put the worksheet in a place where you can see it every day. This will further reinforce your determination to reach your goals. Having the worksheet visible will make the budgeting process much more real to you, encourage you to stay the course, and help you focus on the end results: your written goals and a solid financial future. Frame the sheet if you must to emphasize its importance to you.

Review your goals every year. Delete the ones that you have already achieved or which are not relevant anymore. Add new goals and re-prioritize existing ones. Again, calculate the monthly equivalent dollar amounts by priority. Add up the number-one goals, and your total will be the new amount you need to set aside each month for the coming year.

Sample 1 shows the financial goals for Jane and John Couple. Jane and John are a typical medium-income couple with a ten-year-old daughter, Suzie. They both work full time outside the home. During the last few years, they have accumulated a credit card debt of $7,000, and paying it off is one of their number-one-priority goals, because they feel the interest rates on the cards — 18 percent and 16 percent respectively — are excessive. They also have another number-one-priority goal, that of saving an extra $2,500 to have on hand for family emergencies.

SAMPLE 1: FINANCIAL GOALS WORKSHEET

FINANCIAL GOALS WORKSHEET

Name: __Jane & John Couple__

Date: __April 24, 20--__

Description of Goal	$	How long will it take?	Priority (*)	Monthly Amounts
1) Pay off credit debt	7,000	2 yrs	#1	292
2) Pay off car loan	10,000	3 yrs	#2	278
3) Save an extra $2,500 a year	2,500	1 yr	#1	208
4) Pay down mortgage by extra $10,000	10,000	4 yrs	#4	208
5)				
6)				
7)				
8)				
9)				
10)				

Signature _Jane Couple_

Signature _John Couple_

(*) **Assigning priority:**
"#1" - very important (Total monthly amount $ 500)
"#2" - important
"#3" - not so important
"#4" - nice to have

Jane and John have one number-two-priority goal — to pay off the car loan of $10,000 as quickly as possible. Their car is a one-year-old Chevrolet, and its value today is about $12,000. They estimate that by the time the car loan is paid off, they will be due to trade in their car for a newer vehicle.

The couple have one number-four-priority goal — a goal that falls into the "nice to have" category. They bought their home three years ago, owe their bank a 25-year mortgage of about $100,000, and would like to pay down their mortgage by an extra $10,000 by the time the mortgage is due for renewal in four years' time.

With determination, careful budgeting, and some common-sense spending habits, Jane and John are confident they will achieve their goals. They are on their way to a more secure financial future. Already they're feeling great for having taken the first steps in managing their financial affairs.

Now it's your turn to sit down and do the same.

The next chapter deals, step by step, with putting your budget together.

2

THE BUDGET

Have you ever wondered exactly where your money goes? Or been surprised at how little money you have left at the end of the month, even though you know you're making a decent living? If you answered yes to either or both of these questions, the following exercise should be a real eye opener. This chapter concentrates on getting you to become aware of your spending and outlines a step-by-step method you can use to track your money — on a daily, weekly, monthly, and even yearly basis — and by which you can identify and control your spending habits.

Tracking Spending

Identifying your current spending pattern is an important step in mastering your finances. Once you understand your spending pattern, you will be better able to plan your spending more efficiently to meet the financial goals you set for yourself in Chapter 1. In fact, tracking spending is so important that you will make it your *first* step in your personal budgeting process. (You will discover how to track your income later in this chapter.)

To begin tackling your spending, print the following worksheets from the PDF files on the CD-ROM:

❋ Daily Spending Worksheet

* Weekly Spending Worksheet
* Yearly Spending Worksheet

If you are filling in the forms by hand, you will also need —

* a calculator (or preferably an adding machine with a tape feature),
* a pencil and an eraser for your calculations, and
* a quiet, well-lit work space.

If you work onscreen using the Excel forms on the CD-ROM, all totals will be automatically calculated.

---

tip: Before you can draw up an effective budget, you must become aware of your spending habits.

Daily spending

We spend money each day, often without giving it much thought. We particularly don't think about the small purchases we make, such as the daily lattes and muffins, metered parking, or the occasional magazines we pick up at the grocery checkout counter. Nonetheless, at the end of each month, we find ourselves wondering why we're always left with so little money.

Your personal success in financial budgeting lies in knowing where your money has disappeared to. You will be amazed to see how those cups of coffee can, by the end of the year, add up to the equivalent of one major purchase. The purpose of tracking your day-to-day expenditures is to help you identify your daily spending pattern: to find out exactly how much money is flowing out of your wallet and where it all goes on a *daily* basis.

The Daily Spending Worksheet is designed to help you easily trace your daily spending. Print enough copies of the worksheet for each day of the week, because you'll be carrying one copy with you each day for seven days. If you're part of a couple living in the same household, your partner also should carry one copy per day for the same seven-day period, tracking his or her own spending. Although not necessary, it is preferable to start this exercise on a Monday.

This worksheet lists the common spending categories (or expenses) for a household; for instance, groceries and sundries, coffees and snacks, gasoline, child care, etc. Whenever you make a purchase, find the appropriate spending category and record the dollar amount on that line. You need not bother with the pennies; just round your purchases to the closest dollar. There is space on the worksheet for up to nine purchases in the same spending category for each day. Any purchase you make that does not really fit into a listed spending category can be recorded on a blank line at the bottom of the page; simply identify and record what these purchases are in the first column. Sample 2 is the completed Daily Spending Worksheet of Jane Couple, and will give you an idea of what your own worksheet may look like at the end of the day.

Do not alter your spending habits during the week that you are completing the Daily Spending Worksheets. Continue using cash, checks, and credit and debit cards as you normally would. The only purpose of this exercise is to record all your purchases and write down how much you're spending.

At the end of the day, when all your purchases are recorded, you should add across the page for each spending category to get a total for how much money you spent in that category. Record each category's total in the "Daily Total" column, which is the last column on the sheet. Then add down the "Daily Total" column to arrive at the total spent for the day. You may be shocked by how much you spend in a single day.

Repeat this process for six more days.

If you and a partner are working through this exercise as a couple, each of you should independently record his or her daily spending on his or her own Daily Spending Worksheets. (Be sure you've printed enough copies of the worksheets for both of you.)

A look at Sample 2, the Daily Spending Worksheet for Jane Couple, shows that —

1) in the category "Groceries & sundries," Jane made six purchases totaling $37 for the day;

2) in the category "Household supplies," she made three purchases totaling $7;

SAMPLE 2: DAILY SPENDING WORKSHEET

Day: <u>One (Monday)</u>   **DAILY SPENDING WORKSHEET**

(make 7 duplicate copies)

Spending Category	#1	#2	#3
Groceries & sundries	10	4	7
Household supplies	2	3	2
Pet care & supplies	10		
Coffee & snacks	3		
Take-out & restaurant meals	10		
Wine, beer & liquor			
Haircuts/care			
Cosmetics & toiletries	20		
Other personal care			
Clothing/shoes for self			
Clothing/shoes for family			
Clothing/shoe care & repairs	5		
Gasoline	30		
Car repairs & maintenance			
Parking & tolls	5		
Public transportation & taxis	1		
Other auto & transportation			
Movie rentals	5		
Concerts, plays, sports events			
Event souvenirs, popcorn, etc.			
Hobbies, books, magazines, newspapers			
Lotteries	5		
Other recreation			
Health club visits			
Medical & dental care			
Prescription drugs			
Eye care & other medical			
Child care	20		
Gifts for family & friends			
Children's allowances			
Other spending:			
- *donation/UNICEF*	10		
- *cigarettes*	6		

SAMPLE 2: Continued

Name: __Jane C.__

<!-- (add #1-#9) -->

#4	#5	#6	#7	#8	#9	Daily Total
5	6	5				37
						7
						10
						3
						10
						0
						0
						20
						0
						0
						0
						5
						30
						0
						5
						1
						0
						5
						0
						0
						0
						5
						0
						0
						0
						0
						20
						0
						0
						10
						6
						0
						0
						0
						$174

(transfer to Weekly Spending Worksheet)

3) in the category "Take-out & restaurant meals," she purchased lunch at work for $10;

4) in the category "Movie rentals," she rented a movie on her way home from work for $5; and

5) in the categories "Lotteries" and "Cigarettes," she bought lottery tickets totaling $5 and cigarettes totaling $6. (Note that the item "Cigarettes" does not fit into a listed spending category; therefore, Jane identified it on a blank line at the bottom of the page under "Other Spending.")

Altogether, Jane spent $174 on Day One. She used a combination of cash and credit cards to make her purchases.

Although it's not shown, John Couple (her partner) also completed a Daily Spending Worksheet on the same day.

Weekly spending

Now that you have seven completed Daily Spending Worksheets, it's time to move on to the Weekly Spending Worksheet. This worksheet is designed to help you summarize the daily totals for each spending category from your seven completed Daily Spending Worksheets and see how much you have spent for the week in each category. Completing the Weekly Spending Worksheet will help you appreciate how repeated small purchases add up and how much impact they have on your total spending. This will give you an idea of how your current spending pattern will begin to look over the course of a year.

Print the PDF format Weekly Spending Worksheet that is on the CD-ROM, and refer to it as you read these instructions.

The Weekly Spending Worksheet has two parts. The first part summarizes the category totals from each of your seven Daily Spending Worksheets, giving you a total for each category for the week. The second part takes these weekly totals and helps you determine what all this spending adds up to in a year, using a frequency table. By the time you have worked through the Weekly Spending Worksheet, you will understand the concept of spending frequency, in which you must decide how often a certain type of spending occurs. Your awareness of spending frequency will aid you in budgeting your money. For example, let's say you spent $30 in total this week on your child's school supplies. You anticipate you won't need to spend any more in this category for another month. Therefore, your spending frequency for this category is "Monthly."

Use the following steps to complete page one of the Weekly Spending Worksheet. If you are part of a couple, print an extra copy of the Weekly Spending Worksheet for your partner, which he or she will complete separate from you.

If you are comfortable working with Excel spreadsheets, you may choose to do this exercise on the computer using the Weekly Spending Worksheet in Excel on the CD-ROM. Otherwise, use the PDF worksheet and use a calculator.

1. Transfer all the totals from your Daily Spending Worksheets to page one of the Weekly Spending Worksheet. There are seven columns (Day 1 through Day 7) to accommodate all amounts for each category from the "Daily Total" column of each of your Daily Spending Worksheets. You now have a summary of all your daily spending for the week on one sheet.

2. Total across each line on page one of the Weekly Spending Worksheet by adding up all seven days' spending and recording it in the "Week Total" box for each spending category. (You will find the "Week Total" column is the last column on the right on page one of the worksheet.)

3. Transfer the total spending for each "Day" from the Daily Spending Worksheet.

4. Total the bottom line across to arrive at the total spending for the week.

Take a look at Sample 3, the Weekly Spending Worksheet completed by Jane Couple. Note the following:

1. To fit the pages of this book, each page of the worksheet has been spread over two pages. Refer to the PDF form for the actual layout.

2. The numbers in the first column shaded in gray were transferred from her Day One (Monday) Daily Spending Worksheet (see pages 16 and 17).

3. Jane spent a total of $1,227 for the week.

SAMPLE 3: WEEKLY SPENDING WORKSHEET (Page 1)

Name: Jane C.

(from Daily Spending Worksheets) Spending Category	(Mon) Day 1	(Tue) Day 2	(Wed) Day 3	(Thu) Day 4	(Fri) Day 5	(Sat) Day 6	(Sun) Day 7	Week Total
Groceries & sundries	37			8		75		120
Household supplies	7					20		27
Pet care & supplies	10					15		25
Coffee & snacks	3	4	4	5	4			20
Take-out & restaurant meals	10		30			50		90
Wine, beer & liquor	0					20		20
Haircuts/care	0					25		25
Cosmetics & toiletries	20					5		25
Other personal care	0					12		12
Clothing/shoes for self	0					75		75
Clothing/shoes for family	0					75		75
Clothing/shoe care & repairs	5				20			25
Gasoline	30				25			55
Car repairs & maintenance	0					65		65
Parking & tolls	5	5	5	5	5			25
Public transportation & taxis	1							1
Other auto & transportation	0							0

SAMPLE 3: (Page 1) Continued

(from Daily Spending Worksheets)	(Mon)	(Tue)	(Wed)	(Thu)	(Fri)	(Sat)	(Sun)	
Spending Category	Day 1	Day 2	Day 3	Day 4	Day 5	Day 6	Day 7	Week Total
Movie rentals	5						10	20
Concerts, plays, sports events	0		5		80			80
Event souvenirs, popcorn, etc.	0				20			20
Hobbies, books, magazines, newspapers	0	5				20		25
Lotteries	5		5			7		17
Other recreation	0				10		30	40
Health club visits	0	30						30
Medical & dental care	0							0
Prescription drugs	0							0
Eye care & other medical	0							0
Child care	20	20	20	20	20			100
Gifts for family & friends	0					30		30
Children's allowances	0				5			5
Other spending								
- donation/UNICEF	10							10
- cigarettes	6	6		6	6	6		30
- summer basketball camp for Suzie					100			100
- children's school supplies/activities		15	20					35
Column Total	$174	$85	$89	$44	$295	$500	$40	$1,227

SAMPLE 3: (Page 2)

Spending Category	Week Total	Frequency	Multiplier	Yearly Total
Groceries & sundries	120	weekly	52	6,240
Household supplies	27	monthly	12	324
Pet care & supplies	25	monthly	12	300
Total groceries & household				6,864
Coffee & snacks	20	weekly	52	1,040
Take-out & restaurant meals	90	weekly	52	4,680
Wine, beer & liquor	20	monthly	12	240
Total eating out				5,960
Haircuts/care	25	every 6 weeks	9	225
Cosmetics & toiletries	25	monthly	12	300
Other personal care	12	monthly	12	144
Total personal				669
Clothing/shoes for self	75	every 2 months	6	450
Clothing/shoes for family	75	every 2 months	6	450
Clothing/shoe care & repairs	25	semi-monthly	24	600
Total clothing/shoe				1,500
Gasoline	55	semi-monthly	24	1,320
Car repairs & maintenance	65	every 3 months	4	260
Parking & tolls	25	weekly	52	1,300
Public transportation & taxis	1	weekly	52	52
Other auto & transportation	0			
Total transportation				2,932

Frequency Table

Frequency	Multiplier
	x
Weekly	52
Bi-weekly	26
Semi-monthly	24
Monthly	12
Every 6 weeks	9
Every 2 months	6
Every 3 months	4
Every 4 months	3
Twice yearly	2
Yearly	1

SAMPLE 3: (Page 2) Continued

Spending Category	Week Total	Frequency	Multiplier	Yearly Total
Movie rentals	20	weekly	52	1,040
Concerts, plays, sports events	80	monthly	12	960
Event souvenirs, popcorn, etc.	20	monthly	12	240
Hobbies, books, magazines, newspapers	25	weekly	52	1,300
Lotteries	17	weekly	52	884
Other recreation	40	monthly	12	480
Total entertainment				**4,904**
Health club visits	30	monthly	12	360
Medical & dental care	0			
Prescription drugs	0			
Eye care & other medical	0			
Total health care				**360**
Child care	100	weekly	52	5,200
Gifts for family & friends	30	monthly	12	360
Children's allowances	5	weekly	52	260
Total children & family				**5,820**
Other spending:				
- donation/UNICEF	10	monthly	12	120
- cigarettes	30	weekly	52	1,560
- summer basketball camp for Suzie	100	yearly	1	100
- children's school supplies/activities	35	every 2 months	6	210

(transfer to Yearly Spending Worksheet)

Frequency Table

Frequency	Multiplier
	x
Weekly	52
Bi-weekly	26
Semi-monthly	24
Monthly	12
Every 6 weeks	9
Every 2 months	6
Every 3 months	4
Every 4 months	3
Twice yearly	2
Yearly	1

4. Jane spent the most money on Day 6, Saturday ($500), and the least money on Day 7, Sunday ($40).

Once you've completed page 1 of your Weekly Spending Worksheet, it's time to work with page 2. This is where spending frequencies come into play. Complete page 2 using the following steps:

1. Copy the amounts from the "Week Total" column on page 1 to the "Week Total" column on page 2.

2. Refer to the Frequency Table on page two of the worksheet, then review each spending category and decide how often you feel each expenditure occurs. Record the frequency in the "Frequency" column on page 2. For example, if you spend $20 on a haircut every month, you will record this expense as "Monthly." It is common for spending to occur weekly, bi-weekly, semi-monthly, monthly, every six weeks, every two months, every three months, every four months, twice yearly, or yearly.

3. Once again, refer to the Frequency Table. Notice that each frequency has a corresponding multiplier. Record the multipliers for each spending category in the "Multiplier" column of the worksheet.

4. Multiply the "Week Total" column amounts by the "Multiplier" column numbers. Record your answers in the "Yearly Total" column of the worksheet on the same line.

5. Finally, notice that the spending categories have been arranged into groupings. (For example, the categories "Groceries and sundries," "Household supplies," and "Pet care & supplies" make up the grouping "Total groceries and household.") Add up each spending category in a group to get the total for that group and record these in the "Yearly Total" column. Note that the boxes for grouping totals are outlined in bold type. (These are the amounts that you will transfer to your Yearly Spending Worksheet when the time comes.)

Now, take a look at Sample 3, page 2, Jane Couple's Weekly Spending Worksheet. Note the following:

1. Jane spends $6,864 a year for the family's "Total groceries and household."

2. She spends $4,904 a year for the family's "Total entertainment."

3. Child care, Suzie's allowance, plus other family gifts cost Jane $5,820 ("Total children & family") a year

4. Jane's haircuts cost her $25 every six weeks, or $225 a year. (That's roughly about nine haircuts a year.)

Now that you've completed the Weekly Spending Worksheets, you understand how much you're spending and exactly what you are spending it on, on a weekly basis. You are also starting to get a picture of your spending over the course of a year. It's time to move on to the Yearly Spending Worksheet.

---

tip: Creating a summary of how you are spending your money over the course of a year is an important step in taking control of your finances.

Yearly spending

The Yearly Spending Worksheet summarizes your spending for a year. That is, it tells you how much of your money you are parting with over the course of a year, based on your current spending pattern. This can be an important dose of reality as you decide how to manage your finances. This worksheet includes the numbers you have already calculated and recorded on your Weekly Spending Worksheet, as well as other information you will gather from your bank statements, canceled checks, and credit card statements.

Refer to the Yearly Spending Worksheet, which you can print from the PDF folder on the CD-ROM, or use the Excel worksheet if you prefer to work onscreen.

To complete the Yearly Spending Worksheet, you will need to locate and assemble all your bank statements and canceled checks from at least the last two months. You will also need to locate and assemble all your credit card statements from at least the last two months.

Note: This worksheet can be used by a single householder or by a couple. If you are single, transfer the totals from the Weekly

Spending Worksheet directly to the "Household Yearly Total" column. If you are completing the sheet as part of a couple, you and your partner should transfer the totals from your respective Weekly Spending Worksheets to the columns marked "Partner A Total" and "Partner B Total." Add the two sets of numbers together to arrive at the "Household Yearly Total" amount.

Complete the Yearly Spending Worksheet by following these steps:

1. Review the "Yearly Total" column on page two of your Weekly Spending Worksheet. Transfer the total numbers of each grouping to the "Weekly spending totals" section of the Yearly Spending Worksheet.

2. Examine your canceled checks, bank statements, and credit card statements to complete the next section of the worksheet, "Monthly payments." Notice that this section includes those payments you make monthly, such as mortgage or rent, cable, and telephone. *These payments have not been included in either the Daily Spending Worksheet or the Weekly Spending Worksheet.* Notice also that you are only to include credit card charges not yet included in your other worksheets. (Typically, these charges will be automatic monthly charges and interest expenses.) Do not include your payments to the credit card companies as those amounts have already been accounted for in your Daily and Weekly Spending Worksheets.

3. Once you have identified and recorded all "Monthly payments," multiply each of these by 12 to get yearly totals. Record these totals in the "Household's Yearly Total" column on the same line in the "Monthly payments" section.

4. Complete the last section of this worksheet, "Other payments." This section requires you to list all the other payments you can think of (such as property taxes or insurance) that you pay only once or twice a year and which have not been included above or in any earlier worksheet. Make certain you record only their yearly amount.

5. When you've recorded all the "Household's Yearly Total" amounts in the right-hand column, add up all the figures in that column.

You now know how much you or your household spends in a year.

Sample 4 is the Yearly Spending Worksheet completed by John and Jane Couple. Note the following:

1. The numbers in the column shaded in gray were transferred from page 2 of Jane's Weekly Spending Worksheet (see pages 22 and 23). The column on the right shows the amounts transferred from John's Weekly Spending Worksheet.

2. Jane and John's combined household spending for the year is $65,189 (see page 29).

Jane and John were shocked to discover how much they actually spend in a year. However, they now appreciate how their spending can add up and why they have no money left at the end of the month. Most important, they now have a basis for changing their spending habits.

In Chapter 3, you will learn how to change your spending habits by trimming back your lifestyle rather than cutting out altogether the things you enjoy. But there are still two important aspects of budgeting to explore before moving on: tracking your income and calculating your net worth.

| **tip:** | Remember: Any change in your spending habits must be based in reality. |

Tracking Income

In the previous exercises, you have truthfully calculated your current spending. The next step in your personal budgeting process is to do the same with your income. It is important for you to accurately track your income from all sources, including miscellaneous income such as yearly bonuses, periodic benefits, and interest income. Doing so will help you identify the amount of money you have to work with and will help you focus realistically on how you should adjust your spending to reach your financial objectives.

The Income Worksheet will help you identify, estimate, and list how much money you or your household brings in each year. Tracking

SAMPLE 4: YEARLY SPENDING WORKSHEET

Weekly Spending	Jane C. Total	John C. Total	=	Jane & John's Yearly Total
- Total groceries & household	6,864	2,200		9,064
- Total eating out	5,960	400		6,360
- Total personal	669	800		1,469
- Total clothing/shoes	1,500	1,000		2,500
- Total transportation	2,932	1,200		4,132
- Total entertainment	4,904	400		5,304
- Total health care	360			360
- Total children & family	5,820			5,820
- Other spending:				
- *donation/UNICEF*	120			120
- *cigarettes*	1,560			1,560
- *summer basketball camp for Suzie*	100			100
- *children's school supplies/activities*	210			210

Monthly payments	Jane & John's	x 12	Jane & John's Yearly Total
Mortgage or rent payments	800		9,600
Gas, electricity, oil	75		900
Water, sewage, garbage collection	35		420
Cablevision	50		600
Telephone, cellular & Internet	120		1,440
Car loan or car lease payments	350		4,200
Alimony & child support payments			0
Loan payments to John's dad	200		2,400

SAMPLE 4: Continued

Monthly payments	Jane & John's	x 12	
Student loan payments			0
Consumer loan or line of credit payments			0
Credit card #1 - interest & service charges	45		540
Credit card #2 - interest & service charges	45		540
Credit card #3 - interest & service charges			0
Health insurance			0
Other monthly payments:			0
- condo maintenance fees	150		1,800
- bank charges	25		300

Other payments		
Property tax		700
Home & contents insurance		350
Car insurance, license & registration		1,200
Life, disability insurance		700
Annual health & dental care		500
Membership dues		
Annual vacations		2,000
Other yearly payments:		

Yearly spending total for the household	$65,189

(to Revised Spending Worksheet)

your income is much easier than tracking your spending and will take less time to do. To make the process as smooth as possible, be sure you have on hand all the information and documents listed below.

If you prefer to work with paper and pencil, print the Income Worksheet from the CD-ROM. If you work onscreen using the Excel forms on the CD-ROM, all totals will be automatically calculated.

You will also need —

* all your bank statements and paycheck stubs for at least the last two months;
* all your tax returns for at least the last two years;
* all your investment account statements for at least the last year (but no more than three years).

Now you're ready to complete the worksheet:

1. Record all known monthly income sources in the correct income categories. Review all your bank statements and passbooks to make sure no sources are missed. If you are single, you can ignore the "Partner's Income" columns and just enter your figures in the "Household Monthly Income" column. If you are part of a couple, you and your partner should complete this worksheet together. Each of you should fill in your respective Partner A and Partner B columns, and then add these amounts to arrive at the "Household Monthly Income" total.

    Multiply the "Household Monthly Income" column figures by 12 and record the answers in the "Household Yearly Income" column.

2. If you receive sporadic income payments, estimate your yearly receipts for these items and enter the amounts in the "Household Yearly Income" column.

3. Review your previous years' tax returns to make sure you have not overlooked unusual income such as bonuses and royalties.

4. Review your investment account statements to make sure you have a fair estimate of your yearly investment income.

Yearly investment income includes such items as earned interest and dividends.

> **tip:** Compare an accurate total of your spending to an accurate total of your income, and then decide how you will reach your financial goals.

Sample 5 is the Income Worksheet completed by Jane and John Couple. Note the following:

1. Jane and John both work outside the home and together bring in a total of $5,320 a month in after-tax income.

2. Jane also receives a monthly child tax benefit of $110 from the government for their daughter, Suzie.

3. John and Jane have very little in savings and estimate their yearly interest income to be about $60.

4. John and Jane's total household income for the year is $65,220.

Compare John and Jane's yearly household income — $65,220 — to their yearly household expenditure — $65,189. Already it's evident why they have so little money left over each month, and why they are able to save so little. Even more obvious is the fact that they must change their habits if they hope to reach their financial goals.

You too may find yourself in this position, or worse yet, that you're spending *more* than you make. Don't despair. In Chapter 3, you will learn ways to deal with these situations. For now, the next step is to get an accurate picture of exactly where you stand financially at this moment.

Calculating Your Net Worth

How much are you worth? In dollar terms, what is your net value today? And if you had to make a comparison between your financial situation today and your situation as it will be 12 months from now, or as it was 12 months ago, would you know how to go about doing it? This section will take you through a process called the net-worth calculation, and it will give you the answers to these questions.

SAMPLE 5: INCOME WORKSHEET

Income category	Jane C. Monthly Income	John C. Monthly Income	=	Jane & John's Monthly Income	x	Jane & John's Yearly Income
					12	
Take-home pay (after taxes & deductions)	2,570	2,750		5,320		63,840
Interest & dividend income		5		5		60
Pension income				0		0
Government benefits	110			110		1,320
Alimony & child support income				0		0
Business income (net drawings)				0		0
Rental income				0		0
Miscellaneous & other income:				0		0
Total income	$2,680	$2,755		$5,435		$65,220

Date prepared: April 26, 20—

Net worth is defined as the total dollar value of everything you own (your assets) minus the total dollar value of everything you owe (your liabilities). It is important that you calculate your net worth, as doing so will give you a picture of how much you are worth today and will provide you with a starting point in your money measurement.

Calculating your net worth allows you to objectively measure how you are doing financially over a period of time. For example, let's say you calculate your net worth on January 1 to be $50,000. Then on December 31 of the same year, you once again calculate your net worth, and find that it has increased to $55,000. That means you have improved your personal financial picture by $5,000, either by way of increasing what you own or decreasing what you owe, or a combination of both. Think of how encouraging it would be to have a factual measure of improvement in your finances — and by the same token, how convenient it would be to know that such a calculation can act as an indicator that changes must be made, and that the very information derived from this calculation can assist you in deciding how such changes can be made. (For further discussion, see Chapter 3.)

If you've never done it before, figuring out your net worth may take a bit of time. But if you gather all the necessary papers and use the Net Worth Worksheet provided on the CD-ROM, you can make the process fairly painless for yourself. And it'll certainly be easier when you repeat the process a year from now.

In addition to the Net Worth Worksheet, you will also need —

* a calculator (or preferably an adding machine with a tape feature), unless you are working onscreen using the Excel file,
* all your most current bank statements, and
* all your most current credit card statements.

As applicable, you will need —

* all your most current broker and investment account statements;
* all your most current retirement savings account statements;
* all your most current pension account statements;

* all your most current bank and car loan statements;
* all your most current tax owing statements;
* all your most current student loan statements;
* all your most current mortgage statements;
* your most current cash-value life insurance statement; and
* an itemized listing of your valuables and properties with their fair market value (separate the listings by the type, such as furniture, antiques, jewelry, furs, coin collections, china, silverware, etc.); and
* an accordion-style file folder.

 tip: The net worth calculation is really a comparison of what you own versus what you owe.

Take your time. You are doing important work. Don't rush. Take a break — or two — if you need to.

Start to calculate your net worth by doing the following:

1. Take a close look at all the papers you have gathered. Put them into two piles — an "Asset" pile and a "Liability" pile. The "Asset" pile will comprise papers that show the value of things you own. Examples are your bank account statements for accounts that are not overdrawn, your broker and investment account statements, your cash-value life insurance statement, and itemized listings of valuables. The "Liability" pile will show the opposite, the value of what you owe. Examples of things you'll place in the "Liability" pile are your credit card statements, your mortgage statement, your bank loan statements, car loan statements, and bank account statements for any accounts that are overdrawn.

2. Date the Net Worth Worksheet. It is important to record the date for which your net worth was calculated, because when you calculate your net worth again, you'll be able to make comparisons and get the view of your evolving financial picture. Note that the date you put on the worksheet is not the actual date on which you did the work; rather it is the date on which your net worth is based. It is best to pick a date

such as December 31, September 30, June 30, or March 31, as these are the quarterly dates when most financial institutions provide statements of your accounts.

3. Fill in the values of the "Asset" items on the worksheet, using all the available account statements. In the case of life insurance policies, include on the worksheet only the *cash value* of the policies. (Do not include the benefit amount; that will belong to your beneficiaries, not to you.)

When you come to such items as your home or your car, for which there are no statements, estimate their fair market value based on your knowledge of the current market (real estate or automobile) and the economy. Fair market value means what you think you can sell them for today. Use the most recent appraised value or, in the case of your home, check with your local realtor. You can use the classified section of a newspaper to check for current value on other asset items. You must be realistic, but you don't have to be precise. You will never know what the true values of these items are until they are actually sold.

4. Fill in the amounts of the "Liability" items on the worksheet, using all the available account statements. These are the debts you owe various creditors, including credit card companies, your bank, and your Aunt Martha who loaned you some money. Don't overlook the debt you may owe to the tax department. (Consider it a top priority in your payment plan.)

5. Divide the accordion file into two sections. Label the sections "Assets" and "Liabilities." File your asset-type statements and papers in the "Assets" section, preferably in the same order as you listed them on the Net Worth Worksheet. Do the same with the liability-type statements and papers.

6. Total up your asset items on the worksheet.

7. Total up your liability items on the worksheet.

8. Calculate your net worth by subtracting the liability total from the asset total.

SAMPLE 6: NET WORTH WORKSHEET

As at (date): March 31, 20--

Assets (what you own)	
Bank	
- Checking accounts	535
- Savings accounts	500
- Term deposits	
- Other savings	
Investments	
- Stocks & bonds	5,000
- Mutual funds	
- Other investments	
Retirement savings	22,100
Company pensions - cash value	12,000
Life insurance - cash value	
Real estate	
- Home	150,000
- Rental real estate	
- Other real estate	
Automobiles	12,000
Furniture and appliances	5,000

Liabilities (what you owe)		Interest Rate (%)
Credit card debt	3,000	18
	4,000	16
Personal loans from bank		
Personal loans from others		
Car loans	10,000	9
Mortgage	100,000	8
Student loans		
Income tax debt		
Other loans		
- Loan from John's dad	2,400	12
Total Liabilities (2)	**$119,400**	

SAMPLE 6: Continued

Assets (what you own)	
Personal valuables	
- Jewelry	3,000
- Silverware, china & stemware	1,000
- Collectibles	500
Other asset items	
Total Assets (1)	**$211,635**

(1) subtract (2)		
Total Assets (1)		211,635
subtract	-	
Total Liabilities (2)		119,400
equals	=	
NET WORTH		**$92,235**

Date prepared: April 26, 20–

To see how net worth can act as a financial snapshot, look at Sample 6, the Net Worth Worksheet completed by Jane and John Couple. Note the following:

1. John and Jane have total assets of $211,635.

2. They have total liabilities (debts) of $119,400.

3. Their net worth is $92,235.

4. Their home is worth $150,000 with a mortgage of $100,000 still owing.

5. Their credit card debt totals $7,000.

To increase their net worth, John and Jane will have to either bring more value into their household or pay down their credit card debt and/or mortgage. If they calculate their net worth again six months from now, they'll understand how much — and in what ways — their financial picture has changed.

And how do you feel about your own net worth? Does your picture look positive or negative to you? Don't despair if the initial statement looks disappointing; just keep calculating your net worth from time to time as you continue to practice savvy financial budgeting. You're sure to see some positive changes in your financial picture. All the effort you've put in so far is worth it.

If you've tracked your spending and income and calculated your net worth, you now have something you were lacking before you started: a realistic grasp of your finances. You are now ready to develop a strategy to control your spending and even begin to build up some savings.

3

SPENDING MANAGEMENT

By the time you're ready to tackle the worksheet in this chapter, you should have completed your Financial Goals Worksheet, Daily Spending Worksheets, Weekly Spending Worksheet, Yearly Spending Worksheet, Income Worksheet, and Net Worth Worksheet. You now know how much you are spending per year, how much you are bringing home, how much you are worth, and, most important, you have decided what your financial goals are.

You have probably also realized that to meet these goals, you will have to make some adjustments to your spending patterns, and perhaps to your lifestyle. Don't panic! Even the smallest changes can make a big difference. This chapter focuses on helping you identify what those changes should be, and how you can make them as painlessly as possible.

Analyzing and Revising Your Spending

Start by reviewing your Financial Goals Worksheet. Add up the monthly amounts of the goals you've marked as number-one priorities, and you'll have the total monthly savings you will need to accumulate to achieve these goals. (Once you've achieved your number-one priorities, you can begin saving for your number-two priorities, then your number-three priorities, and so on.) Understand that you must work on your goals one month at a time.

Remember, Rome wasn't built in a day. Be patient and you will achieve your goals.

It's time to think about trimming your expenses, but keep in mind that you may not have to entirely cut out any particular type of spending. Instead, just cut back a little at a time.

For example, instead of driving to work five days a week and paying $10 a day for commercial parking, take the $4-a-day public transit two days a week. You'll save yourself $6 a day for each day you do this. That's $12 a week, or more than $600 a year!

Here's another example. Instead of smoking a pack of cigarettes every two days, reduce your smoking to a pack every three days. That's cutting back just about three cigarettes a day, yet you'll save yourself approximately 60 packs of cigarettes a year. At $6 a pack, that's a total saving of $360 per year!

Small amounts *do* add up. When you're trimming your spending, every category counts. A dollar here and two dollars there will bring you that much closer to realizing your financial goals. Trim your spending by just $5 a day, seven days a week, for a period of one year, and you'll save $1,800!

You can see how dramatic the results are if you save just $5 a day. If you take into account the interest you can earn on $1,800 year after year, the results are even more surprising. (Chapter 5 will cover this topic — the magic of compounding.) You are now learning to be smart with your money.

The following exercise is designed to help you trim your spending. Print the Revised Spending Worksheet from the CD-ROM; note that this is a two-page worksheet, so print both pages before you begin.

You will also need —

* your completed Yearly Spending Worksheet;
* your completed Weekly Spending Worksheet;
* your completed Financial Goals Worksheet;
* a calculator (or, preferably, an adding machine with a tape feature);
* a pencil and an eraser for your calculations and writing; and
* a quiet, well-lit work space.

Note that if you work onscreen using the Excel spreadsheets, all totals will automatically be calculated.

Follow these steps to complete the Revised Spending Worksheet:

1. From your Yearly Spending Worksheet, take the amounts from the "Household's Yearly Total" column and copy these numbers to the "Current Yearly Spending" column on page one of the Revised Spending Worksheet.

2. From your Financial Goals Worksheet, copy the "Total Monthly Amount" of your number-one-priority goals to box (A) on the bottom of page one of the Revised Spending Worksheet.

3. Calculate the yearly amount you must save to achieve your goals by multiplying box (A) by 12. Record the answer in box (B).

4. Now take your Weekly Spending Worksheet and review all the Spending Categories you have carefully recorded. Also look at the amounts for each grouping in the "Yearly Total" column. Highlight (or circle) the spending categories and groupings in which you feel your expenses can be reduced. Ask yourself where you can realistically trim back, and by how much. Then use page two of the Revised Spending Worksheet to note and explain any possible cutbacks you can make in your spending. The "Notes Ref." column on page two of the Revised Spending Worksheet will refer you back to the same line item on page one. For example, if you decide that you can trim $500 a year on "Total entertainment" spending by renting movies only once a week instead of twice, write that down on page two and "Notes Ref." it to "6." This amount of savings ($500) in the "Yearly Savings" column on page one is then listed as "Notes Ref. 6."

5. Continue in this manner until you've completed both pages of the Revised Spending Worksheet. Make sure you cross-reference the two pages under the "Notes Ref." column.

6. Add up the "Revised Yearly Spending" column and the "Yearly Savings" column.

SAMPLE 7: REVISED SPENDING WORKSHEET (Page 1)

(from Yearly Spending Worksheet)	Current Yearly Spending	Revised Yearly Spending	Yearly Savings	Notes Ref.
- Total groceries & household	9,064	8,158	906	1
- Total eating out	6,360	4,800	1,560	2
- Total personal	1,469	1,319	150	3
- Total clothing/shoes	2,500	2,500	0	4
- Total transportation	4,132	3,612	520	5
- Total entertainment	5,304	4,184	1,120	6
- Total health care	360	360	0	7
- Total children & family	5,820	5,820	0	8
- Other spending:				9
- *donations*	120	120	0	10
- *cigarettes*	1,560	780	780	11
- *summer basketball camp for Suzie*	100	100	0	12
- *children's school supplies/activities*	210	210	0	13

Monthly payments:

	Current Yearly Spending	Revised Yearly Spending	Yearly Savings	Notes Ref.
Mortgage or rent payments	9,600	9,600	0	14
Gas, electricity, oil	900	810	90	15
Water, sewage, garbage collection	420	420	0	16
Cablevision	600	480	120	17
Telephone, cellular & Internet	1,440	840	600	18
Car loan or car lease payments	4,200	4,200	0	19
Alimony & child support payments			0	20
Retirement loan payments	2,400	2,400	0	21
Loan payments to John's dad			0	22

SAMPLE 7: (Page 1) Continued

(from Yearly Spending Worksheet)	Current Yearly Spending	Revised Yearly Spending	Yearly Savings	Notes Ref.
Other consumer loan or line of credit payments			0	23
Credit card #1 - interest & service charges	540	540	0	24
Credit card #2 - interest & service charges	540	540	0	25
Credit card #3 - interest & service charges			0	26
Health insurance			0	27
Other monthly payments:			0	28
- condo maintenance fees	1,800	1,800	0	29
- bank charges	300	180	120	30
			0	31
			0	32

Other payments:

	Current Yearly Spending	Revised Yearly Spending	Yearly Savings	Notes Ref.
Property tax	700	700	0	33
Home & content insurance	350	325	25	34
Car insurance, license & registration	1,200	1,100	100	35
Life, disability insurance	700	700	0	36
Annual health & dental care	500	500	0	37
Membership dues			0	38
Annual vacations	2,000	2,000	0	39
Other yearly payments:			0	40
			0	41
			0	42
			0	43
			0	44
Total	$65,189	$59,098	6,091	
	(A)	(B)		

Monthly Savings (from Financial Goal(s) Worksheet) | $500 x 12 = $6,000

SAMPLE 7: (Page 2)

	Notes Ref.
J & J will reduce their groceries & household by 10% by shopping once a week, buying on sale and in bulk, and buying fewer prepared foods.	1
Jane will cut back her coffee expense to $10/wk (from $20); eating out limit to $70/wk (from $90)	2
J & J to reduce their haircuts from once every 6 weeks to once every 2 months.	3
J & J will bike to work one day a week and save $10 in parking & public transportation	5
J & J will reduce their entertainment expense by $1,120 — concerts & plays once every 2 months (from once a month); scale back on lottery ticket purchases to $10 a week (from $17).	6
Jane to cut back on her smoking to $15 a week (from $30).	11
Reduce the use of electricity, heat & gas by 10%.	15
J & J to trim back their cable package by $10	17
The family will limit cellular, extra phone features & long distance calls to $70 per month (from $120).	18

SAMPLE 7: (Page 2) Continued

	Notes Ref.
Negotiate a package deal of $15 per month with the bank.	30
J & J found that they were over-insured for property content and car insurance. They are now insured for less for their property content and have increased their car's deductible to reduce the insurance premiums.	34, 35

7. Rework the numbers until your "Yearly Savings" total is within at least $100 of the amount in box (B), which is the amount you need to trim to meet your financial goals.

You now have a plan for meeting your goals.

Sample 7 is the Revised Spending Worksheet completed by Jane and John Couple. Note the following:

1. Jane and John have explained on page 2 of the worksheet how they will trim their spending in various categories.

2. Jane has always wanted to quit smoking. The desire to revise her spending to meet her financial goals will be an added incentive to her to cut back and eventually quit.

3. Jane and John's number-one priority goals total $500 a month, or $6,000 for the year.

4. By simply cutting back (and not cutting out) their spending, they are confident they will save $6,091 in the coming year and meet their financial goals of paying half their credit card debt and saving an extra $2,500. Furthermore, they will have $91 left over!

5. In addition to paying the interest on their monthly credit card statements, Jane and John will pay off $292 a month of their credit card debt. They will be paying off the credit card with the highest interest rate first.

6. They will also put $208 a month into their emergency-fund savings account. Jane and John may choose to defer this $208-a-month saving for the first seven months, and redirect the money toward paying down the credit cards first. This will increase their credit card payments to $500 a month for seven months. Then they will put the $500 a month into savings for the remaining five months in interest-paying, short-term deposits. By paying down the credit cards first, they will reduce their credit card interest expense for the year.

Jane and John must be careful not to incur new credit card debt while they trim their spending. By being disciplined, Jane and John will, in two years' time, pay off their credit card debt and have an extra $5,000 in savings. This new habit will also save them $1,200 in credit card interest thereafter and will increase their overall net worth by $12,000!

You can make the same sort of improvement in your own financial health by simply revising some of your spending patterns. To make it easier for you, try the following:

* *Pay yourself first.* Each month, put the amount you plan to save into an account of its own. If you don't have the money to spend, you won't spend it.

* *Equalize your spending.* Opt to pay your bills on a monthly basis wherever possible. Expenses such as insurance and property tax can be more easily managed if payments are made each month. Make certain, however, that you are not paying extra for this payment option.

* *Consider stretching your intervals of spending.* For example, instead of buying a pack of cigarettes every day, buy one every day and a half. Get your hair cut once every seven weeks instead of once every six weeks. Use a window-cleaning service every six months, rather than every four months. Try grocery shopping every nine days instead of every seven days. Have take-out lattes and coffees only twice a week instead of four times.

* *Continue tracking your spending.* Keep an eye on your spending to make sure it continues to stay within your revised budget.

You'll find even more tips on saving money in Appendix 2.

But what if you've trimmed and cut back and crunched the numbers as much as you can but still can't come up with a revised spending plan that works? Read on. The next section deals with how to make the best of your situation if you cannot save enough to meet your financial goals.

Changing Your Lifestyle

Perhaps you've discovered that revising your spending isn't enough. What should you do now if you cannot meet your financial goals, no matter how realistically you've trimmed your spending on the Revised Spending Worksheet?

There are three very clear-cut solutions to this dilemma:

1. Sell some things you own (your assets) and use the money to pay down your debt; and/or

2. Downsize your lifestyle moderately; and/or

3. Earn more income.

> **tip:** You may have cash tied up in things you don't use. Look at your possessions and determine what you can do without. Do the same for the services for which you pay.

Take a close look at your completed Net Worth Worksheet. Review the list of the things you own under the "Assets" section on the left side of the page. Which items can be sold off or downsized? How much extra cash can you net from their sales?

Also examine the "Liabilities" section on the right side of the page. With the extra cash from the sale of your assets, could you eliminate or reduce some of the items on your liabilities list? Keep in mind that most debts have interest costs. By eliminating or reducing the debt, you will also eliminate or reduce the related interest.

It may be difficult for you to visualize how your family can make do with only one car instead of two, or how to make up your mind to sell the family's SUV and buy a used Honda Accord, or sell the wide-screen TV and other fancy electronics. But remember: You must be realistic about your lifestyle. Not everyone should have all the consumer goods that advertisers insist you must have. At best, these items are merely nice to have, and only if you can afford them.

Get rid of things you don't need. Sell them in the classifieds of your local newspaper or at an auction. Have a garage sale. Turn these items into cash and pay down your debt or put the money into savings. Downsizing your lifestyle doesn't necessarily mean that you're going to have to do without forever. You just have to do without for now.

Move to a smaller home and pay less in rent or mortgage payments. Trophy homes cost! Cancel the high-end fitness club membership and join the neighborhood gym. Don't try to keep up with the Joneses. Forget about what others have. You don't need the latest, the fastest, or the biggest. Buy only what you need, not everything you want.

Keep in mind that ads and commercials are designed to sell you *exactly what you don't need*. You can never keep up with the latest gadgets, and, often, as soon as you buy something, it's out of date. If you must buy something, no-name-brand items are frequently just as good as brand-name items, and come without the high price tag.

Finally, it may be necessary for you to work harder to meet your goals. Consider taking another job to earn more money. Think about working six days a week instead of five, or taking on a part-time evening or weekend job. It may be necessary only for six months or so, but if it can help you get over a money crunch, it's worth doing.

Focus strongly on your financial goals. Do you really want to keep the two cars when the consequence of doing so is being saddled with that $10,000 student loan that you cannot pay off? Do you need the home theatre when you have $8,000 in credit card debt, carried at an interest rate of 18 percent? Do you need to live in a 3,000-square-foot house with a mortgage that eats up 50 percent of your paychecks? Moderate your lifestyle and remove the money stress in your life. Stick to your financial goals.

---

tip: Let your financial goals become your motivation for keeping to your revised budget.

Let's review what you have accomplished so far by following the advice in this book. You have —

* identified realistic financial goals you want to achieve;
* tracked your current spending patterns;
* tracked your income patterns;
* identified what you own and what you owe;
* looked hard at your spending and trimmed as much as you can to save for your goals; and
* looked at other means to improve your financial picture, including selling assets, downsizing your lifestyle, and earning more money.

You are now well on your way to financial peace of mind and freedom. You have learned that saving money is not so difficult a task if you start by being aware of where you spend your money, then trimming back a little. You've learned that you can change your lifestyle to one of lower consumption without sacrificing your quality of life. When you see your financial goals — in writing, every day — you have a reason (or many reasons) to stay focused.

You've realized that nobody is going to do it for you. You are responsible for whatever goals you've set for yourself. Respect yourself and your decision. *Be confident that you can succeed.* Take comfort in knowing that you can achieve any financial goal or goals you set your mind to, because you now have the means and skills to do it and you have it on paper! You have control over your money; you know money does not control you.

You also know that determination and patience pay off and in the end will bring you long-term financial security and help you realize your lifelong dreams, one step at a time.

Keeping your new budgeting resolution in mind, you're now ready to tackle other financial challenges. Chapter 4 is devoted to the lesson of debt management. It covers credit card and mortgage management, and it takes a closer look at the credit rating process.

4
DEBT MANAGEMENT

It can be very difficult to avoid debt. Credit cards, consumer loans, and mortgages are a part of the way we live today. Almost everyone will need to take out a mortgage in order to buy a home. Many of us will sign up for a loan to purchase a car. Most of us obtain credit cards for buying convenience and for identification purposes.

You must understand debt, or it can become a source of misery and stress. Debt comes in two forms: good and bad. "Good" debts are loans taken out to purchase appreciating and/or income-producing assets. One example might be a mortgage taken out to help purchase a rental property. "Bad" debts are loans taken out for consumption. For example, if you charge your Disneyland holiday on your credit cards and you don't have the money to pay for it when the bills arrive, this is "bad" debt.

This chapter concentrates on ways to manage your debt — eliminate "bad" debts first, then pay down the "good" ones. Ultimately, your aim is to have as little debt as possible.

Paying Off Your Consumer and Credit Card Debts

Credit cards from department stores, gas companies, and the like fall into the category of consumer credit cards. Visa and MasterCard fall into the category of popular credit cards. Both types usually charge a high rate of interest on any unpaid balance that you carry. If you are unable to pay off your balances on time every month, chances are you are paying too much interest to the credit card companies. These companies are only too happy to have you pay them just the minimum amount indicated on the monthly statements, because they can continue to charge you an exorbitant interest rate on the outstanding balances.

Consumer loans are just as bad as credit cards. These are loans taken out to purchase items like appliances and furniture. Consumer loans usually come with a high interest rate to make up for consumers who have been and continue to be guilty of nonpayment. If you have one or more of these loans, it is in your best interest to pay them off as quickly as possible. You should treat these loans as you would credit card debt: Get rid of them fast.

It may not seem like much when one of your credit cards charges you $15 a month in interest. But if the balance you owe them is $1,000, you are effectively paying an 18 percent rate of interest on this debt. Let's say you owe a total of $5,000 on all your credit cards, at that rate of interest, and you pay off only the interest portion of the debt each month. Your total interest expense will be a whopping $900 a year! Imagine what you could do with $900 if you didn't have to pay it to the credit card companies.

Consumer credit cards usually charge the highest interest rates on lending, so you would be wise to pay them off first before paying off other types of debt, and to pay them off as quickly as possible. Look at your monthly credit card statements — every one of them should indicate the current rate of interest you are being charged on the outstanding balance you owe.

> **tip:** Credit card debt is a source of great misery for many people. Eliminate it, and you've eliminated a source of stress.

The total of all unpaid credit card balances should be listed on your Net Worth Worksheet as a liability item. It may take you a few years to pay off the credit card debt, but remember that it probably took you just as long to accumulate the amount you owe. Keep in mind, too, that as you pay down your credit card debt, your overall net worth increases. Be patient: You can whittle down the debt one card at a time. Your plan is to pay off the credit card with the highest interest rate first, then the next highest, and so on, until all outstanding balances are gone.

Using the following techniques, you can control and reduce your consumer and credit card debt:

* *Pay with cash*. Until you can control your spending, always pay with cash for anything you buy.

* *Have fewer cards*. Keep only one or two major credit cards. Cut up the rest. Do not sign up for any new cards.

* *Get a lower rate*. If you are carrying a balance, look for a credit card that offers a lower interest rate and transfer other credit card debt to that card. Shop around: different credit cards offer different terms and conditions. Make sure you read and understand the fine print.

* *Pay according to the rate*. Pay off your most expensive credit cards first.

* *Consolidate your debts*. Consider a debt consolidation loan to reduce your interest payments. Use the loan to pay off the credit cards and other consumer loans immediately, and cut up those cards! Do not start charging again. Then focus on paying off the consolidation loan.

* *Use your savings*. Consider cashing in any term deposits or other savings you may have to pay off these debts. It is unlikely that your term deposits are earning you the high rate of interest that the credit card companies are charging you. Don't forget to build up your savings again as soon as you can, and cut up those cards. You should not have any card that charges you more than 15 percent interest a year.

* *Save to buy*. Save for a purchase instead of buying it with credit. It's incredibly easy to pay for something with a credit card, but much harder to do it with real money.

* *Think before you buy anything*. Do you really want to be paying for that restaurant meal a year after you've consumed it? And with interest?

Paying Down Your Mortgage

If you own your own home, chances are there's a mortgage attached to that home. Over the life of a typical mortgage (usually about 25 years), the majority of the payments you make will be on the interest portion of the mortgage. For example, the interest portion alone on a mortgage of $100,000 over 25 years at an interest rate of 7 percent would be more than $110,000! That means you would pay a total of $210,000 for a $100,000 mortgage.

Although it is a good debt — one that helps you acquire an appreciating asset — it's still to your advantage to pay off your mortgage as quickly as possible. The shorter the life of the mortgage, the less interest you will pay and the more money you will have in your pocket. If you currently have a mortgage, periodically assess whether it would be wise for you to refinance. Keep an eye on interest rates. Do the same thing if your mortgage is up for renewal soon.

You may be able to use the following methods to pay off your mortgage sooner than you'd planned — and save lots of interest in the process:

* *Take out a mortgage with a shorter amortization period.* Instead of a 25-year mortgage, consider a 20-year or even a 15-year mortgage if you qualify and can afford the increase in payment amounts. Table 1 uses the example of a $100,000 mortgage at 7 percent:

Table 1 Mortgage Savings

Amortization Period	Monthly Payments	Total Interest	Total Savings
25	$700	$110,000	
20	$770	$85,000	$25,000
15	$895	$61,000	$49,000

* *Look for a mortgage that allows you to make payments more frequently.* If you can make payments on a weekly or bi-weekly basis, you'll end up paying off your mortgage earlier, thus saving yourself thousands of dollars in interest.

* *Watch for tax deductible payments.* Keep tabs on the mortgage interest you have paid as you can deduct it from taxable income in certain circumstances. Use the resulting tax savings to fast-track your mortgage payments. (Note: US and Canadian tax laws differ on deductibility of interest. Check the law for your country.)

* *Shop for the best mortgage rate available.* Even a quarter or a half of one percentage point will save you thousands of dollars in interest over the life of the mortgage. Lending institutions include commercial banks, trust companies, credit unions, mortgage companies, home builders and developers, and government housing agencies.

* *Use a mortgage broker.* They often can shop for the best rate on your behalf. Mortgage brokers are usually paid by the lending institution, so there should be no additional cost to you.

* *Look for partial prepayment options and take advantage of them.* If your mortgage allows you to make lump-sum payments or increase your monthly payments, take advantage of these options to shave interest off your total mortgage.

* *Consider refinancing your mortgage.* This will work in your favor if you can refinance at a lower rate and/or better terms, and if the institution at which you have your current mortgage will not charge you a huge penalty for retiring your mortgage early.

* *Consider a variable-rate mortgage.* If you believe interest rates will remain stable or move downward in the next few years, this is a good option. Variable-rate mortgages have no fixed interest rate; the rate simply fluctuates with the market. When the market rate goes up, the interest rate on your mortgage will also go up. If the market rate goes down, so too does the rate on your mortgage. Banks usually charge a lower rate of interest on variable-rate mortgages because they are not taking any risk on rate fluctuations — you are.

* *Be wary of mortgage insurance offered by your lending institution.* Often it is too expensive. Instead, take out the same amount in life insurance to cover the value of your mortgage. You can save on premiums over the life of the mortgage if you reduce this coverage as you pay down the mortgage.

Your Credit Report

Somewhere out there in the world of money, bill payments, credit card debt, loans, and mortgages, there's a credit report with your name on it. This ever-evolving document contains all kinds of information about your financial standing, and it also rates your credit-worthiness. That notion alone may be unsettling, but the truly scary part is that any potential lender can access your credit report and read your credit rating.

Do you know your credit rating? Were you even aware that there's a credit rating report on you out there, and have you ever seen it? How does the rating process work? Read on. Your credit rating can have a direct impact on your financial health, and it pays to understand the rating process.

Your credit rating is established at the time when you have your first credit application approved. The application may be for a credit card, a car loan, a mortgage, or some other form of consumer debt. To maintain a good credit rating, pay back the money you have borrowed or use your credit card and pay the bill on time. You must also pay your other bills (such as utility and telephone bills) on time. You can damage your credit rating by paying your bills late, missing a payment, not paying at all on the debt you owe, or by not keeping up with your other bills. Keep in mind that your credit rating (bad or good) stays on your record for quite a long time — often for as long as ten or more years.

tip:	Your credit rating can have enormous influence on your life. Do what you can to ensure that it's healthy.

Other information that goes on your record includes —

* your personal data such as your birth date, social security number or social insurance number, current and previous addresses, and your employment history;

* inquiries made by credit grantors and others who may extend a loan to you;

* any collections and delinquent information;

* any bankruptcy information;

* any judgments, foreclosures, liens, and garnishments against you; and

* any credit counseling consumer proposals to creditors.

You can obtain a copy of your credit report online or by writing to the reporting agency or bureau (common ones include Equifax, TransUnion, and Experian; see the Resources listed on the CD-ROM for their website addresses). Along with your request for a copy of your report, include your name, current and previous addresses, birth date, social security number or social insurance number, your signature, and a photocopy of two pieces of ID containing your signatures. There is usually a small fee charged for this service.

The report will list your credit history with all reporting creditors, assigning you a rating by number from each of them that indicates your creditworthiness. These ratings indicate how responsible you have been in relation to your credit with that particular creditor. For example, a "1" rating means you have paid your bills within 30 days; a "2" rating means that you have paid in 31–60 days (one payment behind); and so on up to a "9" rating, which means a collection agency is involved in trying to collect your account. A "0" rating means you are too new to rate yet but credit has been granted to you.

When you receive your credit report, review it carefully. Errors in reports do sometimes occur, and if an error is serious enough, you may find it almost impossible to obtain credit until the error is corrected. This could put you in a real bind if you are in a situation in which you need credit immediately, such as getting your student loan approved for school next fall.

If, when you get your report, you do find errors, note these down and contact your creditors immediately. Have them correct their mistakes and have them notify the credit bureau so that your credit record can be updated with the accurate information. Finally, follow up with the credit bureau to make certain the corrected information is, in fact, in place.

If you find yourself with a poor credit rating, don't despair. You can improve it by doing the following things:

- Start paying your bills on time. This positive action will be reflected on your credit report.

- Do not apply for more credit. Remember that every credit application request will show up on your report. This is one case in which less is best.

- Stay put. Do not move for at least four years or longer. Stay in your current job as long as possible. Staying put is interpreted as a sign of stability.

- Request notations be put on your record to explain unusual circumstances, or statements to counter unfavorable and erroneous ratings. An example may be a note from you stating, "The Sears account was closed in 2004 and the balance is paid off."

It's important that you check your rating periodically, preferably on a yearly basis. There have been cases of fraud committed in respect to credit information. Unknown to you, someone may be out there claiming to be you and systematically destroying your creditworthiness.

No one but you is responsible for your credit rating. Be vigilant. Pay your bills on time and check periodically to make sure the information in your credit report is accurate.

Take the time to understand the credit-rating process and take action now. You'll feel more confident and more in control of your life. You'll also feel more positive about your creditworthiness and not have to constantly worry about your poor credit rating.

As you can see, debt management is important to your financial well-being. When your debt is under control, you can look forward to the next step in financial planning: the process by which you accumulate savings and let your savings make more money for you. The next chapter takes you into the realm of growing your dollars.

5

SAVINGS MANAGEMENT

Let's say you've managed to tame your debt and are now beginning to accumulate some savings. Just imagine: For the price of a cup of coffee at your neighborhood coffee house each day, you can accumulate wealth up to six figures! Impossible, you say? But reality says it can be done.

You've heard the phrase "the magic of compounding," and you've also heard that you can "put your money to work for you." This chapter discusses some simple but effective investment basics.

Relax. Smart savings management is a skill that can be learned, and the rewards for doing so can be very satisfying.

More to Savings than Savings Accounts

You, like many other people, may have a natural tendency to put any extra money you have into a savings account. While the urge to save is a good one, you may not be doing yourself any favors if you leave your money in a savings account for long periods of time without paying close attention to the interest that money can earn while it's in the account. When it comes to your savings, there are a number of investment instruments from which you can choose other than just a savings account. In fact, savings accounts offer one of the lowest rates of return on your money of any investment instrument, and you would be wise to park your savings there on only a temporary basis.

To save successfully, you must invest your hard-earned dollars wisely so that they begin to generate income for you. Instead of immediately spending the income from your investments or savings, allow it to accumulate. This is called earning income on your income. This simple method of wealth accumulation is probably the most popular, painless, and powerful way to save. Most millionaires did not, in fact, gain their wealth from inheritance, gambling, or lottery winnings. They earned it by working hard and making their savings work equally hard. Over time, you'll be amazed how money can literally make money for you. In today's investing environment, it is not unusual to earn an average return of 8 to 10 percent from your investments.

Take a look at Savings Chart 1 in Appendix 1. If you can save $1,000 a year for 20 years and invest this money each year at a 6 percent after-tax rate of return, you can expect, in the twentieth year, to make $2,207 in income from these savings! Continue this way for another ten years, and your savings will bring you $4,743 in income in the thirtieth year! That's more than double the twentieth-year income.

Imagine, now, what could happen if you save $2,000 a year instead of $1,000. Your income in the twentieth year will double to $4,414, and in the thirtieth year will increase to $9,486! We are certainly not talking pennies here. This is often referred to as the "magic of compounding." Anyone can do it. All you need is patience and a bit of perseverance.

Keep on imagining. Not only has your income on your investment grown year by year, but your total savings have also ballooned to some impressive numbers. In the twentieth year, your savings total $38,993; and in the thirtieth year, $83,802. And all because you saved $1,000 each year and let the money work for you! To put this in even simpler terms, we're talking about a saving habit of just $19.23 a week, or $2.75 a day! (That's probably less than the price you pay for your daily latte.)

Before you start saving and investing, though, there are some basics you must understand:

* There's a risk/return trade-off
* There are different types of investments for your savings —

- → safety investments
- → income investments
- → growth investments

* There are different types of income —
  - → interest income
  - → dividend income
  - → capital gains
* There are mutual funds
* There are real property investments

Risk/Return

You should know the basic rule of the game: the higher the risk involved in a savings or investment instrument, the higher the expected rate of return. For example, investing in a US or Canadian government bond is safer than investing in a corporate bond. This is because there is more risk associated with holding a corporate bond than there is with holding a government bond. North American government bonds are guaranteed by their respective governments, and the chances of these governments defaulting on a bond (that is, not paying you back for your investment) are slim. Because of their relative safety, they pay you a relatively low rate of interest for holding the bond.

Conversely, you would expect a higher rate of interest to be paid to you if you decided to take on the added risk that comes with holding a corporate bond. These bonds are not guaranteed by any governments. If the company goes under, you may not recover your investment.

There are literally hundreds of different types of investments into which you can put your savings, and they all have their own risk level. You should take the time to thoroughly understand these instruments before investing in them. Be honest with yourself about your own level of risk tolerance, and invest accordingly.

Different Types of Investments

What follows here are brief descriptions of each of the more common investments.

Safety investments

These are generally available in US and Canadian dollars. They are relatively short-term, usually less than one year before maturity. They are issued by banks, credit unions, and governments. Safety-type investments include —

* savings accounts with your bank or credit union,
* short-term certificates of deposit,
* short-term treasury bills, and
* money-market funds.

Safety investments are considered safe because they usually offer you a certain rate of interest and are guaranteed by a bank, credit union, or government. They can be cashed fairly quickly, and there's very little risk of you not getting your money back. But these investments also offer you the lowest rates of return. They are ideal instruments for you to use if you need to park your money somewhere temporarily. For example, you've got $1,000 in your checking account, and you don't need to use this money for bill payments for another two weeks. You may want to transfer this excess cash into a money-market fund and earn some interest while it's sitting idle. You transfer the money back into your checking account when it's time to use it for bill payments.

Money-market funds are pools of very short-term investments in which you can participate. They are "highly liquid," meaning you can transfer your money in and out of these funds very quickly. Most of these funds require only one day's notice to cash them in and out. You will earn interest for the time period your money is in the pool.

Income investments

Income-type investments are so called because they earn you mainly interest income. In essence, you loan your money to either governments, banks, or corporations, for a period of usually 5 to 20 years. In return for the use of your money, the borrowers promise to pay the loan back to you on a stated date and also promise to pay you regular interest. Because of the additional risk you take on in this type of investment, the interest rates are higher than those associated with the safety-type investments. Common income-type investments include —

* government bonds,
* guaranteed investment certificates (GICs),
* corporate bonds, and
* strip bonds.

When you invest in fixed-rate GICs, you should negotiate with your bank for the best rate by asking the institution for the maximum rate they will offer you in order to get or keep your business. Don't be shy; you won't know until you ask!

Certain government and corporate bonds may also be bought and sold on the open market prior to their maturity dates. You can make or lose money by doing so. Money you make on the sale is called capital gains. Money you lose is called capital losses.

Another type of income investment is dividend income from preferred stocks that you own. Dividend income is different from interest income. When a company pays you a dividend, it is essentially paying you a share in the company's profit, since you are part-owner of the company through holding its preferred stocks. Preferred stocks are issued most frequently by blue-chip (that is, large and well-established) corporations, and are called this because holders of preferred stocks rank ahead of common stockholders in their claims on a company's assets. Preferred stockholders rank behind creditors and bondholders. Most investors buy preferred stocks for their regular payment of dividend income, and these investments are viewed as being more secure because they are usually issued by very large, stable corporations. In addition, when you sell preferred stocks, you'll have either capital gains or losses, depending on whether you made or lost money on the transaction.

Growth investments

The most common growth-type investments are common stocks and preferred stocks (which were touched on in the previous section).

Preferred stocks represent partial ownership in a company. Most preferred stockholders have no voting rights. As already mentioned, these stocks are considered a safer investment than common stocks. Preferred stockholders rank ahead of common stockholders in claims on the company's assets, which becomes important if the company in which the stock is held fails.

Common stocks also represent partial ownership in a company. Most common stockholders have voting rights. However, should the company fail, common stockholders rank last in payment, behind creditors, bondholders, and preferred stockholders (in that order). Common stockholders have no right to demand dividend payments since payments are declared and paid only at the discretion of the company's board of directors. Because of the added risk associated with owning common stocks, investors expect a higher rate of return for investing in them.

There are different types of common stocks:

1. *Blue-chip common stocks.* These are common stocks of large, well-established, and reputable companies that have a history of profitability and dividend payments. Blue-chip stocks offer the potential for you to earn capital gains when you sell your stocks, and earn dividend income while you hold them. They are considered the least risky of all common stocks. Examples of blue-chip companies include Proctor & Gamble and Disney.

2. *Growth common stocks.* These are common stocks of companies that have potential for huge growth over time. Such stocks offer potential for attractive capital gains but offer small or no dividends because these companies generally put their profits back into their operations, rather than paying them out to the stockholders. Growth stocks are considered risky investments, and some investors expect to make "a killing" on these stocks. More often than not, though, investors take a huge risk on these stocks and end up holding stocks that have less value than the paper on which they are printed! Examples of growth stocks that turned bad include stocks of start-up mining and high-tech companies.

Mutual funds

Mutual funds are investments you buy to become a stakeholder in a pool or basket of stocks or bonds, or a combination of both. Mutual funds are still very popular with investors. They are sold in units, and normally the price per unit fluctuates on a daily basis, depending on the value of the underlying stocks and/or bonds. Usually, you can buy and sell these units on the open market, just as you would do with stocks.

tip:	Mutual funds are a good investment option for small investors. A mutual fund allows you to spread your money over many different types of investments.

Mutual funds come in the form of one, all, or any combination of the following investments:

* short- and long-term government bonds
* corporate bonds
* mortgages
* treasury bills
* preferred stocks (with emphasis on dividend income)
* blue-chip stocks
* growth stocks
* foreign-government bonds (of many countries around the world)
* foreign stocks (of many countries around the world)

There are many benefits to owning mutual funds:

* *Liquidity*. Most funds are traded on the open market. You can buy and sell them easily and at any time at the prevailing price of the day. You can find these prices in your daily newspapers and through your investment broker.
* *Professional management*. Most people lack the time or skills to continue evaluating their investments in stocks and bonds. Mutual funds have professional managers who make investment decisions on your behalf, within the guidelines established by the fund. In exchange for this service, the fund charges a management fee.
* *Diversification*. A basic principle of sound investing is to avoid putting all your eggs in one basket. Instead of taking your $10,000 savings and investing it in one or two types of

bonds and three different stocks, you can spread the same amount over two different mutual funds, which collectively may hold 25 bonds and 50 stocks. You end up owning less of each, but have the advantage of distributing your money over many different types of investments.

Common types of mutual funds include the following:

* *Bond funds.* Bond funds invest in bonds of different maturity terms, levels of government, and corporations. These funds are considered less risky than equity funds because they earn interest income on a regular basis as well as have the potential to earn capital gains. Bond funds may hold, say, a combination of federal, state or provincial, and municipal bonds in their pools, with terms ranging from 10- to 20-year maturities paying different rates of interest.

* *Equity funds.* Equity funds invest in various stocks — both common and preferred, blue-chip, growth, and even stocks of foreign companies. These funds are divided into different classes: conservative equity funds (which invest mainly in blue-chip stocks of large, well-established companies); growth equity funds (which invest mainly in stocks that offer high-growth potential); and global-stock funds (which invest only in stocks of foreign countries). Equity funds are more risky than bond funds, and of course growth equity funds and global stock funds are more risky than conservative equity funds.

* *Balanced funds.* Balanced funds invest in a combination of bonds and stocks. Their risk level is dependent on the mix of bonds and stocks, as well as the types of bonds and stocks. They are generally more risky than bond funds but less risky than equity funds.

Real estate investment

It is appropriate and prudent to add real estate to your investment portfolio, especially if your portfolio is a sizeable amount. It is not advisable to hold only real estate in your investment portfolio. Rather, it should be part of your total investment package, which should include other investments such as bonds, stocks, and mutual funds. This helps to better diversify your investments and spread out your investment risk. Your principal residence is excluded as a real property investment.

During the period of real property holding, you may even further your profit by renting your holding and generating a positive cash flow. Managing a rental property is no easy feat, especially if you are unlucky enough to inherit troublesome tenants. Nonetheless, it can be worthwhile for those who are willing to take on the risk of long-term real property investment.

> **tip:** A savings account will not allow your money to grow much. To increase your wealth, investigate other investment options.

As you can see, there are many different investment products available to you today for your investing dollars. Venture out of savings-account mode and start exploring and learning about some of these other, highly popular investment options. But always keep this in mind: if you desire a higher rate of return, you must expect to take on more risk. At the same time, appreciate that if you place your money in high-risk investments, you must be prepared for the possibility of losing some or all of what you have put in.

Take your savings and put them into a variety of investments. Buy some GICs, some mutual funds, some individual stocks, and some bonds. This is called investment diversification. Make periodic changes and adjustments to your portfolio to maximize your investments' growth potential, depending on the risk level you're willing to accept.

If you are fairly conservative and cannot handle much risk, the bulk of your investments should be in GICs, government bonds, bond mutual funds, and balanced mutual funds. You may wish to consider investing a small amount in conservative equity and foreign mutual funds.

If, however, you are a risk taker, you may wish to place the bulk of your investments in individual stocks (growth and foreign types) or equity mutual funds, and a small amount in bonds.

Let's go back to the savings scenario discussed on page 60. If you can invest your $1,000-a-year savings to earn you an after-tax return of 8 percent instead of 6 percent, your income from the investment in the twentieth year will be $3,661 (instead of $2,207). That's an increase of 66 percent! Save for another ten years to the thirtieth year, and the income will be $9,063 (instead of $4,743). That's a 91 percent increase! (See Savings Chart 2 in Appendix 1.)

Furthermore, by the twentieth year, your total savings will be $49,423; and in the thirtieth year, $122,346. These are huge numbers — and all from saving just $2.75 a day!

You can appreciate why it's important to manage your savings actively and wisely. Every percentage-point increase on your rate of return will add a huge amount of dollars to your savings over time.

It's time for you to start investing. It's important for you to start investing.

And it's never too late for you to start investing!

The ABCs of Retirement Savings

More and more people are finding themselves responsible for financing their own retirements. They can no longer depend on their employers for pensions to see them through their sunset years. This is due to a number of factors:

* Employers are discovering that they can no longer afford to fund retirement plans for their employees.

* If employers do contribute to their employees' retirement, they often contribute directly into the employees' own individual retirement plans, which the employees themselves are responsible for managing. This strategy relieves the employers of guaranteeing a certain amount of pension to their employees on retirement.

* Many governments, crown corporations, and large, transnational companies have been downsizing, with the result that fewer and fewer employees qualify to join these employer-funded pension programs.

* A greater number of people are now self-employed, and they must take care of their own retirement savings.

Governments in North America have recognized how important it is that their citizens also provide for their own retirement, and so have created tax incentives to encourage the population to save for retirement. The money contributed to a qualified or registered retirement plan is usually tax deductible and tax sheltered until withdrawn. That is, you can deduct the contributions you make to one of these plans against your income for tax purposes, and any income earned from these contributions remains tax sheltered until you withdraw the money. As a result, you have a lower taxable income in the years of contribution and also in future years when these contributions start earning investment income.

Whether you already have a qualified or registered retirement plan or are just starting one, it is important for you to keep a few things in mind:

1. *It's never too late or too early to start.* It is wise to start saving for retirement when you're young; say, in your early twenties, when you first start working. Not only will you get into the habit of saving for retirement, you will enjoy a longer benefit period from the compounding effect on your retirement savings. That is to say, you are letting your money earn more money for you. The rule is that the longer you let your money stay invested, the more money you will end up with in your plan.

   But it really is never too late to start, so don't put it off any longer. Don't give up on the idea of saving at all because you think you are now too old to do so. There are things you can do to catch up. You may not end up with as much money as you would have if you'd started saving early, but you will still have more than you would if you hadn't started saving at all!

   Refer to Savings Chart 2 in Appendix 1. If you put $1,000 a year (that's just $83.33 a month, or $19.23 a week) into your retirement savings account, and on average you earn 8 percent on these investments, in 20 years' time you will have $49,423. If you continue for another ten years (making the time you leave your money invested total 30 years), your savings will total $122,346. That's two and a half times the 20-year amount!

   Now let's say you have only 15 years instead of 30 to save for retirement. You can still catch up by saving more — say, $2,000 a year. Again, refer to Savings Chart 2 in Appendix 1. If you invest this money at 8 percent for 15 years, you will have $58,648 ($29,324 x 2) — which is better, you must admit, than if you did not save at all.

2. *Utilize asset allocation.* When there's a substantial balance in your qualified or registered retirement plan — say, more than $10,000 — investigate allocating the money to different types of investments. Just as there are many types of savings vehicles available (as discussed in the previous section), there are also many types of retirement-savings instruments from which you can choose.

There are the mainstays, such as GICs (guaranteed investment certificates) and term deposits from your bank or credit union. These usually pay a low rate of interest because they are considered low-risk investments. There are also other types of investments, including government and corporate bonds, shares and stocks of publicly traded companies, and mutual funds. Keep in mind that different types of retirement-savings investments carry different risk levels; you should expect to earn higher rates of interest on higher-risk investments. For example, because of the high risk involved in investing in stocks of a start-up company, you would expect to earn a higher rate of interest from doing so than you would from investing in an almost no-risk federal government bond.

The secret to successful retirement saving is to strike an appropriate balance between the various types of investments: some lower risk, some higher risk, and some in-between. Focus on long-term performance rather than trying to time the market. Consider your age when investing. Generally, the closer you are in years to retirement, the less risk you should take with your investments. Remember that you are saving to have funds that will be needed in the future: It is best to stay away from the very high-risk investments. You don't want to gamble with your retirement money.

3. *Invest abroad.* Don't ignore foreign markets. When you are saving for retirement, think about including investments in overseas markets in your portfolio. Although the North American stock markets are sizeable, you should also consider investing in other parts of the world — Asia, Europe, and South America. This type of global diversification is necessary because not all markets move in the same direction as North America's. By investing in these markets,

you can take advantage of their growth when it happens. You should apply this technique to the bonds, stocks, and mutual funds in your retirement-savings portfolio.

4. *Consider borrowing to save for retirement.* It may not be a bad idea to obtain a retirement-savings loan, provided you are committed to meeting the required monthly payments on the loan. Don't forget to apply any tax refund generated by the retirement savings immediately against the loan to reduce the amount owing and save yourself some interest on the loan. This strategy is, in essence, one of forced saving for your retirement, and can be effective.

5. *Lean more toward growth-type investments.* If retirement is far into the future, or you have a high risk-tolerance level (meaning you can sleep at night even when your investments are not performing well), consider moving more of your retirement savings into stock mutual funds and/or individual stocks. Historically, the stock market has produced a better rate of return over time than have other types of investments such as bonds and term deposits. However, investing in growth can mean a bumpy ride, so make sure you can stomach it.

Take a look at Savings Chart 3 in Appendix 1. If you can achieve a 10 percent rate of return over 30 years on savings of $1,000 a year, you will end up with $180,943. This is $58,597 more than the $122,346 earned at 8 percent over the same 30-year period. Of course, you will likely take on more risk at 10 percent than you would at 8 percent.

6. *Continually monitor your retirement-savings portfolio.* It is imperative that your portfolio be actively managed to ensure it has a healthy balance of investments and is invested in both domestic and foreign markets. Know your own risk tolerance and invest accordingly, and as your portfolio grows, do not hesitate to seek professional advice. It is one thing to make a mistake on a $10,000 investment account, but quite another on a $500,000 portfolio! Usually the best advice will come from a registered professional financial planner or accountant.

7. *Don't trade excessively.* Your investments may be eaten up by the commissions you end up paying when you trade excessively in your retirement-savings account. Buy bonds

and stocks that you intend to hold for a long time, such as blue-chip stocks. Look for mutual funds that allow you to switch between funds without a fee.

8. *Don't wait until the last minute to make your qualified or registered retirement plan contributions.* If you procrastinate and wait until the deadline to contribute, it may result in you making quick and poor investment decisions. The best plan is to make regular contribution payments to your qualified pension or registered retirement plan. If you must contribute near or on the deadline, temporarily put the money into a money-market fund. Switch to other, more appropriate retirement-savings instruments after you have given it some thought. But again, do not procrastinate!

Our sample couple, Jane and John, have decided that they want to start saving for their retirement as soon as their credit card debts are paid off, which will be in two years. At that time, they should be able to start putting at least $6,000 a year into their retirement plans ($3,000 for Jane and $3,000 for John).

They also believe, at their moderate risk-tolerance level, that they will be able to earn a rate of return of 8 percent a year. They want to continue contributing for 30 years. Again, following Savings Chart 2 in Appendix 1, Jane and John calculate that their total retirement savings at the end of 30 years will be as follows:

$122,346 (per $1,000 savings) x 6 = $734,076

This lump sum should provide a good return that will adequately supplement the government and employers' pensions, to which they will be entitled when they retire in 30 years.

For more information on retirement and eldercare planning, see *Finances After 55*, also published by Self-Counsel Press. Knowing as much as you can about this subject is essential to your financial health and well-being for the latter part of your life.

6

FINANCIAL PLANNING STRATEGIES

Personal budgeting is only one aspect in your overall financial planning. Retirement planning (discussed in Chapter 5) is another. But there are two other very important areas of financial planning you should consider:

1. Tax planning

2. Estate planning

Tax Planning

It pays to reduce your tax burden. The good news is that there are ways you can do it legally! It's a good idea for you to get some advice on your particular tax situation from a professionally registered accountant and/or financial planner. However, to get you started, here are four basic strategies you can employ:

1. Reduce your taxable income:

   ❖ Take advantage of all available tax deductions.

   ❖ Maximize your tax deductible qualified or registered retirement plan contributions.

   ❖ Consider starting a small business to claim various expenses that are not otherwise available to you.

2. Split your taxable income:

* Pay family members a fair amount for their services in your small business. You can claim this payment as a business expense and deduct it from income. The family member will report the income, and if she or he is in a lower tax bracket than you are, the overall tax burden on the family will be reduced.

* Loan your family members money for investments. Although the initial income may be attributable back to you, subsequent income on income from investments in the family members' hands may eventually be taxed in their hands, hopefully still at a lower rate.

3. Defer your taxable income:

* Qualified or registered retirement plan contributions are a good example of a way to defer taxable income. Tax on contributions to qualified or registered retirement plans is deferred until this money is withdrawn from the plan (which is designed to occur upon retirement). In addition, the income earned on the investment is also deferred until withdrawn.

4. Convert your taxable income:

* Taxation varies depending on the type of investment income you earn. Investment income taxed at 100 percent should be sheltered in your qualified or registered retirement plan, and income taxed at less than 100 percent can be structured in investment accounts outside your tax-sheltered accounts.

Taxation can be a daunting area to venture into, but it's in your best interest to stay informed about your taxation system and understand the options that may be available to you. Whenever necessary, consult a tax professional. This is one area where the rules constantly change. You cannot afford to be ignorant in these matters.

Estate Planning

Now that your financial goals and budget are in place and you're looking at a more secure financial future, you are ready to think about estate planning. Estate planning involves the creation and completion of financial and legal documents concerned with end-of-life issues. Having an estate plan can save your family and loved ones a great deal of anxiety, and maybe even anguish, at a time when they can least cope with it. Proper planning can help to secure their financial futures as you wish them to be, and also minimize the payment of unnecessary estate tax and other final return taxes. The following estate-planning items should be on your things-to-do list:

1. Write out a will and keep it updated, preferably on a yearly basis. If you don't have a will, you give up control over how your estate will be distributed. You give up the right to choose your estate's beneficiaries, to appoint your preferred executor and trustee, to designate a guardian for your minor children, and to make specific gifts to friends and relatives. Another consideration is that changes in tax laws may affect your estate, which may result in your estate paying more taxes and probate fees — and your family being left with fewer of your assets than you wish them to have.

2. Draw up a power of attorney. A power of attorney is a document that gives someone authority to act as your agent on your financial matters should you become incapable of acting for yourself. It is usually set up at the same time as you draft your will. If you are in a stable relationship, you can assign your power of attorney to your partner. If you are not, a trusted relative or friend may be chosen instead.

3. Draw up a living will. Also called an advance directive or a health-care directive, this is a document that states how you wish to be treated, should you become incapacitated by illness, injury, or old age. Your living will covers procedures that may prolong your life but not cure you. Typically, the document requests that —

   * all life-prolonging measures be rendered; or
   * all life-prolonging measures be withheld; or
   * some mixture thereof be rendered; and
   * you be provided with "comfort care," including pain medication.

These directives allow you to make decisions well ahead of your final illness. They also relieve your family of the burden of making painful life and death decisions for you.

4. Take the time to select the right executor for your estate. First ask for that person's permission before naming him or her as the executor of your estate. Your executor should be trustworthy and financially prudent, and should not be likely to predecease you. Keep in mind that the person who accepts the role of executor will be personally and totally liable for your estate's affairs. Consider an alternate executor who can take over if the initial executor named becomes unable or unwilling to act. It may be wise to also consider naming a trust company as your estate's co-executor.

5. Build up sufficient financial resources for your estate's final expenses. These final expenses may include inheritance and other taxes, funeral arrangements, probate fees, money to pay off any and all debts, and other costs of administering the estate after death. Taking out life insurance now to fund these matters in the future may be a consideration.

6. Prepare an up-to-date inventory listing of your assets, debts, and other important papers. You should update this inventory at least once a year. Some of the more important items in this inventory will include —

   * bank accounts (include account numbers and locations),
   * ownership papers (include the deed to your house and other properties),
   * credit card numbers,
   * insurance policy papers,
   * other applicable insurance papers, and
   * location of your safety deposit box.

7. Take time to communicate with your family about your wishes. Include them in the decision-making process when it comes to your estate planning. Doing so will minimize the possibility of a family member challenging your will after your death. Make sure that everyone understands the will and the reasons for your bequests.

8. Take time to learn about estate planning. Read books, attend workshops, and consult with professionals. This field is constantly changing. It is important for you to keep informed of

tax changes and talk to estate- and financial-planning experts on a regular basis.

9. Don't ignore your retirement planning. This should be one of your priorities.

10. Don't ignore life! Do take time to smell the roses. Enjoy your loved ones today.

For more information on wills, powers of attorney, and estate planning, see *Write Your Legal Will in 3 Easy Steps*, the *Living Wills Kit*, and the *Have You Made Your Will?* forms kit, all published by Self-Counsel Press.

Knowing as much as you can about financial planning is essential to your financial health and well-being. It is not a given. It doesn't happen overnight and it doesn't happen automatically. You work at it, and if you follow this kit's advice, you will achieve financial freedom painlessly regardless of how much you earn. It's a matter of changing your outlook on spending and saving.

Live within your means. Once you have your finances in order and know that you've planned to take care of your loved ones, it's time to look at other aspects of your life such as pursuing a life-long interest or hobby. It's time to think about yourself. Doing so is okay, because at this point, you've earned it!

7

FREEDOM TO ENJOY LIVING

True financial freedom does not depend on the amount of money you have. It comes from the knowledge that you have the ability to control and manage your money. Real financial freedom knows no money fears or anxieties.

Regardless of how much money you have or how much money you make, if you don't feel you have enough, you will never be truly free. Freedom comes only when you believe you are rich, at any income level, and in all aspects of your life.

Remember when you first started working part time, while still in high school? Remember that first paycheck? You were excited. It seemed like so much money! You felt rich. Yet the actual amount of that paycheck was probably a pittance compared to what you are making today. Why did you feel rich then and not now? And why did you have money left over for savings then, but not now? The answers to these questions could lie in how you saw your lifestyle then versus how you see it today.

Then, you did not own a car and have to pay for car insurance and gas. You did not eat out in expensive restaurants. You did not buy designer clothes every time you went shopping. Your lifestyle was very different. Now, you have a big house and owe an equally big mortgage. You eat out at least twice a week. You wear designer or trendy clothes. You have your hair done at least once a month. What you may not realize is that in reality, all these habits restrict your freedom.

Stop buying toys and gadgets just because your friends or neighbors have them. Just stop buying stuff. Before you buy something, really think about whether you actually need it, or simply want it. If it's a "want" item and you buy it anyway, it becomes another "bondage" item, especially if you are in debt.

Be content with less. You don't have to eat out or order in twice a week. Economize, and be content with eating out once every week or even once every two weeks. It's a matter of perception. Contentment does not come from your actual quality of life, but your *perception* of quality of life!

Your ultimate revised financial budget (provided you were true to yourself as you worked through it) will provide you with the blueprint for a new lifestyle. Yet the changes you are about to make are small and relatively painless. Get into the new spending and saving patterns, and you won't even know you are on a budget. It will easily become the lifestyle of your future.

As you become accustomed to your new spending habits, you will find that you are more open to other changes. You will look forward to achieving the next goals on your list, and will revise your future financial budgets accordingly. Remember that a financial budget is an ever-evolving entity. You are free to make changes to suit your needs as time goes on. Make it your goal to revisit your budget at least once a year.

Start today. Take control of your finances and start living the simpler and more stress-free lifestyle that you are meant to live.

---

tip: Start today. Start now. Take control.

Appendix 1
SAVINGS CHARTS

SAVINGS CHART 1

Monthly savings: __$83.33__

Yearly equivalent: __$1,000.00__

Interest rate: __6.0%__

Year	Beginning Balance	Annual Savings	Total	Interest Earned	Ending Balance
1	0	1,000	1,000	60	1,060
2	1,060	1,000	2,060	124	2,184
3	2,184	1,000	3,184	191	3,375
4	3,375	1,000	4,375	262	4,637
5	4,637	1,000	5,637	338	5,975
6	5,975	1,000	6,975	419	7,394
7	7,394	1,000	8,394	504	8,897
8	8,897	1,000	9,897	594	10,491
9	10,491	1,000	11,491	689	12,181
10	**12,181**	**1,000**	**13,181**	**791**	**13,972**
11	13,972	1,000	14,972	898	15,870
12	15,870	1,000	16,870	1,012	17,882
13	17,882	1,000	18,882	1,133	20,015
14	20,015	1,000	21,015	1,261	22,276
15	22,276	1,000	23,276	1,397	24,673
16	24,673	1,000	25,673	1,540	27,213
17	27,213	1,000	28,213	1,693	29,906
18	29,906	1,000	30,906	1,854	32,760
19	32,760	1,000	33,760	2,026	35,786
20	**35,786**	**1,000**	**36,786**	**2,207**	**38,993**

SAVINGS CHART 1 — Continued

Year	Beginning Balance	Annual Savings	Total	Interest Earned	Ending Balance
21	38,993	1,000	39,993	2,400	42,392
22	42,392	1,000	43,392	2,604	45,996
23	45,996	1,000	46,996	2,820	49,816
24	49,816	1,000	50,816	3,049	53,865
25	53,865	1,000	54,865	3,292	58,156
26	58,156	1,000	59,156	3,549	62,706
27	62,706	1,000	63,706	3,822	67,528
28	67,528	1,000	68,528	4,112	72,640
29	72,640	1,000	73,640	4,418	78,058
30	**78,058**	**1,000**	**79,058**	**4,743**	**83,802**
31	83,802	1,000	84,802	5,088	89,890
32	89,890	1,000	90,890	5,453	96,343
33	96,343	1,000	97,343	5,841	103,184
34	103,184	1,000	104,184	6,251	110,435
35	110,435	1,000	111,435	6,686	118,121
36	118,121	1,000	119,121	7,147	126,268
37	126,268	1,000	127,268	7,636	134,904
38	134,904	1,000	135,904	8,154	144,058
39	144,058	1,000	145,058	8,704	153,762
40	**153,762**	**1,000**	**154,762**	**9,286**	**164,048**

* This chart assumes a perfect return environment from year to year. It is provided as a guide only.

SAVINGS CHART 2

Monthly savings: ___$83.33___

Yearly equivalent: ___$1,000.00___

Interest rate: ___8.0%___

Year	Beginning Balance	Annual Savings	Total	Interest Earned	Ending Balance
1	0	1,000	1,000	80	1,080
2	1,080	1,000	2,080	166	2,246
3	2,246	1,000	3,246	260	3,506
4	3,506	1,000	4,506	360	4,867
5	4,867	1,000	5,867	469	6,336
6	6,336	1,000	7,336	587	7,923
7	7,923	1,000	8,923	714	9,637
8	9,637	1,000	10,637	851	11,488
9	11,488	1,000	12,488	999	13,487
10	**13,487**	**1,000**	**14,487**	**1,159**	**15,645**
11	15,645	1,000	16,645	1,332	17,977
12	17,977	1,000	18,977	1,518	20,495
13	20,495	1,000	21,495	1,720	23,215
14	23,215	1,000	24,215	1,937	26,152
15	26,152	1,000	27,152	2,172	29,324
16	29,324	1,000	30,324	2,426	32,750
17	32,750	1,000	33,750	2,700	36,450
18	36,450	1,000	37,450	2,996	40,446
19	40,446	1,000	41,446	3,316	44,762
20	**44,762**	**1,000**	**45,762**	**3,661**	**49,423**

SAVINGS CHART 2 — Continued

Year	Beginning Balance	Annual Savings	Total	Interest Earned	Ending Balance
21	49,423	1,000	50,423	4,034	54,457
22	54,457	1,000	55,457	4,437	59,893
23	59,893	1,000	60,893	4,871	65,765
24	65,765	1,000	66,765	5,341	72,106
25	72,106	1,000	73,106	5,848	78,954
26	78,954	1,000	79,954	6,396	86,351
27	86,351	1,000	87,351	6,988	94,339
28	94,339	1,000	95,339	7,627	102,966
29	102,966	1,000	103,966	8,317	112,283
30	**112,283**	**1,000**	**113,283**	**9,063**	**122,346**
31	122,346	1,000	123,346	9,868	133,214
32	133,214	1,000	134,214	10,737	144,951
33	144,951	1,000	145,951	11,676	157,627
34	157,627	1,000	158,627	12,690	171,317
35	171,317	1,000	172,317	13,785	186,102
36	186,102	1,000	187,102	14,968	202,070
37	202,070	1,000	203,070	16,246	219,316
38	219,316	1,000	220,316	17,625	237,941
39	237,941	1,000	238,941	19,115	258,057
40	**258,057**	**1,000**	**259,057**	**20,725**	**279,781**

* This chart assumes a perfect return environment from year to year. It is provided as a guide only.

SAVINGS CHART 3

Monthly savings: ___$83.33___

Yearly equivalent: ___$1,000.00___

Interest rate: ___10.0%___

Year	Beginning Balance	Annual Savings	Total	Interest Earned	Ending Balance
1	0	1,000	1,000	100	1,100
2	1,100	1,000	2,100	210	2,310
3	2,310	1,000	3,310	331	3,641
4	3,641	1,000	4,641	464	5,105
5	5,105	1,000	6,105	611	6,716
6	6,716	1,000	7,716	772	8,487
7	8,487	1,000	9,487	949	10,436
8	10,436	1,000	11,436	1,144	12,579
9	12,579	1,000	13,579	1,358	14,937
10	14,937	1,000	15,937	1,594	17,531
11	17,531	1,000	18,531	1,853	20,384
12	20,384	1,000	21,384	2,138	23,523
13	23,523	1,000	24,523	2,452	26,975
14	26,975	1,000	27,975	2,797	30,772
15	30,772	1,000	31,772	3,177	34,950
16	34,950	1,000	35,950	3,595	39,545
17	39,545	1,000	40,545	4,054	44,599
18	44,599	1,000	45,599	4,560	50,159
19	50,159	1,000	51,159	5,116	56,275
20	56,275	1,000	57,275	5,727	63,002

SAVINGS CHART 3 — Continued

Year	Beginning Balance	Annual Savings	Total	Interest Earned	Ending Balance
21	63,002	1,000	64,002	6,400	70,403
22	70,403	1,000	71,403	7,140	78,543
23	78,543	1,000	79,543	7,954	87,497
24	87,497	1,000	88,497	8,850	97,347
25	97,347	1,000	98,347	9,835	108,182
26	108,182	1,000	109,182	10,918	120,100
27	120,100	1,000	121,100	12,110	133,210
28	133,210	1,000	134,210	13,421	147,631
29	147,631	1,000	148,631	14,863	163,494
30	**163,494**	**1,000**	**164,494**	**16,449**	**180,943**
31	180,943	1,000	181,943	18,194	200,138
32	200,138	1,000	201,138	20,114	221,252
33	221,252	1,000	222,252	22,225	244,477
34	244,477	1,000	245,477	24,548	270,024
35	270,024	1,000	271,024	27,102	298,127
36	298,127	1,000	299,127	29,913	329,039
37	329,039	1,000	330,039	33,004	363,043
38	363,043	1,000	364,043	36,404	400,448
39	400,448	1,000	401,448	40,145	441,593
40	**441,593**	**1,000**	**442,593**	**44,259**	**486,852**

* This chart assumes a perfect return environment from year to year. It is provided as a guide only.

SAVINGS CHART 4

Monthly savings: $83.33

Yearly equivalent: $1,000.00

Interest rate: 12.0%

Year	Beginning Balance	Annual Savings	Total	Interest Earned	Ending Balance
1	0	1,000	1,000	120	1,120
2	1,120	1,000	2,120	254	2,374
3	2,374	1,000	3,374	405	3,779
4	3,779	1,000	4,779	574	5,353
5	5,353	1,000	6,353	762	7,115
6	7,115	1,000	8,115	974	9,089
7	9,089	1,000	10,089	1,211	11,300
8	11,300	1,000	12,300	1,476	13,776
9	13,776	1,000	14,776	1,773	16,549
10	**16,549**	**1,000**	**17,549**	**2,106**	**19,655**
11	19,655	1,000	20,655	2,479	23,133
12	23,133	1,000	24,133	2,896	27,029
13	27,029	1,000	28,029	3,363	31,393
14	31,393	1,000	32,393	3,887	36,280
15	36,280	1,000	37,280	4,474	41,753
16	41,753	1,000	42,753	5,130	47,884
17	47,884	1,000	48,884	5,866	54,750
18	54,750	1,000	55,750	6,690	62,440
19	62,440	1,000	63,440	7,613	71,052
20	**71,052**	**1,000**	**72,052**	**8,646**	**80,699**

SAVINGS CHART 4 — Continued

Year	Beginning Balance	Annual Savings	Total	Interest Earned	Ending Balance
21	80,699	1,000	81,699	9,804	91,50⊂
22	91,503	1,000	92,503	11,100	103,60⊂
23	103,603	1,000	104,603	12,552	117,15⊂
24	117,155	1,000	118,155	14,179	132,334
25	132,334	1,000	133,334	16,000	149,334
26	149,334	1,000	150,334	18,040	168,374
27	168,374	1,000	169,374	20,325	189,699
28	189,699	1,000	190,699	22,884	213,583
29	213,583	1,000	214,583	25,750	240,333
30	**240,333**	**1,000**	**241,333**	**28,960**	**270,293**
31	270,293	1,000	271,293	32,555	303,848
32	303,848	1,000	304,848	36,582	341,429
33	341,429	1,000	342,429	41,092	383,521
34	383,521	1,000	384,521	46,143	430,663
35	430,663	1,000	431,663	51,800	483,463
36	483,463	1,000	484,463	58,136	542,599
37	542,599	1,000	543,599	65,232	608,831
38	608,831	1,000	609,831	73,180	683,010
39	683,010	1,000	684,010	82,081	766,091
40	**766,091**	**1,000**	**767,091**	**92,051**	**859,142**

This chart assumes a perfect return environment from year to year. It is provided as a guide only.

Appendix 2
TIPS ON SAVING MONEY

General

* Buy less stuff!

* Don't be afraid to ask for a discount — nicely. It doesn't cost you anything to ask "Will this item be on sale soon?" or "Will you consider offering me a discount on this item?" or "Can you do better on the markdown?" Just remember to ask politely, and don't be pushy.

* Cut up all but one credit card. Keep it in a safe but remote place so that it is not easily accessible. Use only cash for purchases.

* Pay your bills on time to avoid interest and late-penalty charges. Doing so is especially important for credit card debt and tax bills.

* When you pay your credit card bills, pay them off in full. Some cards will charge interest on all new purchases even if you carry a balance of only a penny on your card.

* Review the interest rates you're currently being charged on all the debt you owe. Pay off the most expensive debt first. Consider consolidating some or all of your debt if you can obtain a loan with a lower interest rate.

* Review your bank charges. If you are paying for debit card charges, take these into account as well. Some banks offer package deals on all your banking needs. Do shop around; bank charges differ tremendously. Compare them in detail.

* Do not give in to impulse buying. Before making a "nice-to-have" purchase, think about it overnight. After you've slept on it, buy only if you really feel strongly about the item.

* If you like shopping, go window shopping for fun but leave your credit and debit cards at home.

* Shop in the off season, especially for clothing and Christmas items. For example, buy fall clothes in the spring and buy summer clothes in the fall. Better labels usually go on sale between Thanksgiving and January.

* Shop with a list. Try not to deviate from it and try to buy things on sale.

* Shop at consignment and secondhand stores. Many items are as good as new, but at a big discount.

* Quit smoking (start by cutting back) and moderate your alcohol consumption. Government taxes are usually exorbitant on these items. You are literally burning up your money when you smoke!

* Cut down on take-out coffees and lattes. These make coffee businesses — and not you — rich!

* Cut down on take-out, eat-out, and home-delivered meals.

* Search the Internet for websites that specialize in e-coupons. You can often find sites that offer coupons valid in your area for various purchases. See the websites listed on the CD-ROM under Resources.

* Buy a good secondhand car instead of a new one. A new car depreciates significantly as soon as you drive it off the lot.

* At the end of each day, put your spare change into a glass jar. At the end of each month, deposit the coins in a separate bank account. By the end of the year, you will be surprised how much money you have saved. Use 90 percent of this money to either pay down your debt or save for your retirement. Don't forget to use the remaining 10 percent to treat yourself.

- Check out your local dollar store and enjoy the mountains of savings.
- Watch less TV, and say no to home shopping channels and buying online. No catalogs in the house. All of those increase the temptation to buy!
- Don't "supersize" your purchases. Buy just enough for consumption, unless it is certain the items will be used at a later date.
- Set a spending limit and stick to it when you go shopping.

Household

- Replace 100-watt bulbs with 60-watt bulbs.
- Buy fewer dry-clean-only clothes.
- Conserve energy and save on your electricity and gas bills. Turn off lights in unoccupied rooms.
- Skip the heat-dry cycle of your dishwasher and air-dry your clean dishes. Always have a full load before doing your dishes or laundry.
- Always reduce the recommended dosage for laundry detergent, bleach, fabric softener, and other cleaning supplies. Your clothes will be just as clean if you use half to two-thirds the amount of detergent and bleach as recommended by the manufacturer.
- Cut fabric-softener sheets in half and use one-half sheet per load. You won't notice the difference and doing this makes the softener last twice as long.
- Dry your clothes in the sun as a real cost saver.
- Try using fewer appliances/machines that heat (dryers, heaters) or cool (air conditioning, refrigerators, freezers). These appliances use more energy (power) than any other appliances.
- Avoid shopping with friends who shop like they are rich.
- Don't bring the kids shopping. Kids will entice you to spend more than you can afford.

* Eliminate mindless extras. From premium level cable service to the deluxe bundling of your telephone service, pare them all down.
* Be careful with bulk buying. It's no saving if you end up throwing half your purchases away.

Personal Care

* Instead of washing your face with expensive facial moisturizing soap or cleanser, try using powdered milk. Add a bit of warm water to it to make a paste before applying it to your face. The gritty texture acts as an excellent exfoliant, and it's mild on your face and makes it feel soft. It's an inexpensive alternative to chemical-laden cleansers.
* Substitute fresh rice water for your astringent. Keep a bit of the water you use to wash your rice and store it in a jar in the fridge. When you want to use it, soak a cotton swab and wipe your face with it. It is an excellent refresher in the summer; use it from a spray bottle. After two days, water your plants with any remaining water, as it contains nutrients beneficial to all living things.
* Dilute your shampoos and conditioners with water to stretch your dollar. You can increase the quantity of these products by about 25 percent by using this technique, without feeling you've skimped on your hair care.
* Check out the local tech school for your haircuts, coloring, or permanents. The costs are a fraction of what a salon would charge.
* Cancel your gym membership if you aren't going frequently. Belonging to a gym is good, but most people don't go nearly often enough to make a membership worthwhile. Instead, do some "free" exercises: walking, running, doing push-ups, or using exercise videos.

Home Office

* Recycle and reuse office paper. Consider using the clean back side of unwanted and nonconfidential paper for draft copies of work that you'll keep in your own files. Not only will you

save money, but you'll also save a tree and help the environment.

* Reassess your magazine and newspaper subscriptions when they come up for renewal. Are they necessary or just "nice to-have" publications? Renew only the necessary subscriptions. Borrow the "nice-to-have" magazines from the library or friends.

Food

* Never go shopping hungry. Try to shop after a full meal.

* Buy as few prepared foods as possible. Try to make meals from scratch. You will not only save money; you'll also be healthier.

* Cut back on junk food.

* Pack your own lunch at least once or twice a week.

* Shop for in-season vegetables and fruits. For example, buy more root vegetables in the winter, as they cost less than exotic vegetables that must be imported from the tropics.

* If you live in a large city, shop in ethnic stores. The prices are usually better.

* Be smart with leftovers. Use them in creative ways to make new dishes. Turkey leftovers from the holiday season can be used in a variety of turkey dishes. Use the meat in stews, stir-frys, salads, and sandwiches. Use the bones to make turkey soup stock.

* Many recipes call for seldom-used, expensive ingredients. Learn to substitute less costly items. For example, a recipe calls for fresh basil leaves, but it's winter and fresh basil is expensive. You can substitute dried basil powder, or even other spices such as oregano or tarragon. Another recipe calls for red wine. You can instead use white wine, beer, chicken stock, or maybe milk, orange juice, or even water. Be creative and flexible.

* Bulk up your meals to make them go further. A little meat can go a long way if you combine it with lots of vegetables and potatoes, rice, or pasta. Bread crumbs can also extend meat dishes such as meatballs, meat loaf, hamburgers, and casseroles.

* Make food in bulk, then freeze it in individual containers for later use.

* Grow your own food (vegetables, herbs, fruits).

* When shopping, look for equivalent no-name or store-brand products. Their quality is usually as good as that of name brands, and you save on the price.

* Avoid buying ready-made sauces or spice mixes. Spend some time learning how to make them yourself. They're deceptively simple, and much, much cheaper.

* Dilute thick sauces and dressings with a bit of water, broth, or juice to make them last longer.

* Don't throw out the syrup from canned fruits — freeze it in ice cube trays. Then, when you are making smoothies, just throw the cubes in the blender instead of using regular ice!

* If you buy bottled water at work every day at $0.75 per bottle and there are 250 working days per year, you are spending over $185 a year! Solution: bring the water from home!

Christmas

When it comes to Christmas, commercialism has won out over the real celebration of the occasion. It's easy to be caught up in the hype and frenzy. There is great pressure on you to overspend on gifts, clothes, home decor, and, of course, food and drink. Here are some tips to help you stay on the saving wagon:

* Make your own personalized gifts. Gift baskets are great. Make your own wines, jams, vinegar, and other craft items.

* Make a list and shop for Christmas items after Christmas and throughout the year when they're on sale.

* Skip the Christmas tree. Alternatives can be as simple as taking large glass vases and filling them with Christmas lighting and decor for a festive display. Group them on tables and counters for impact.

* Skip the Christmas cards. E-mail holiday wishes to as many friends as possible.

* Don't buy gift tags. Cut out pictures from old Christmas cards for use as gift tags. Enlist your kids for this task!

* Recycle gift bags, wrapping paper, ribbons, and bows.
* Encourage a policy in your extended family of only one gift per adult. Draw for the name of the one adult you will be buying a gift for this coming Christmas. Agree on a maximum price limit on the gift. Reserve individual gifts only for those under 16 years of age in the family, and also set a price limit for each child's gift.

Other Occasions or Celebrations

* Do not simply invite family or friends over for dinner. Make the get-together a potluck, and have everyone bring an agreed-on dish, a bottle of wine, or other beverage to the family meal. Not only will it be more economical for you, but you will also actually enjoy the party more because you won't be so overworked.
* Shop for birthday and other presents during the year when items are on sale. The best times of the year include Boxing Day, January, February, and after-season-end periods.
* Re-use decorative gift bags.

Activities

There are many activities you can do as a family that cost little or no money at all.

With Kids

Don't buy into spending a lot to have fun with the kids. Be creative. Here are a few examples you might consider:

* Skip the movies. Pop your own healthy popcorn and rent a couple of videos instead.
* Go hiking and pack a picnic lunch. Decide as a group where to go. Scout out walking trails and routes together.
* When eating out with kids in restaurants, keep in mind that most portions are big enough for two to share. Young children don't eat much anyway, especially when they're excited.
* Look for places where kids under a certain age can be admitted for free when accompanied by an adult.

* Eat in places where kids can eat for free.

For Adults

* Instead of dinner out and a movie, consider dinner out *or* a movie.
* Make your own "theme" dinners at home.
* Go to discounted matinees rather than evening movies. Eat beforehand so you won't be tempted to buy popcorn and drinks.
* Eat and drink during happy hours in pubs and bars. Usually these places offer attractive discounts to entice you to drink more — just don't!
* Be an early-dinner bird. Some eateries offer specially priced dinners if you order before 5:30 p.m. or 6:00 p.m. You get the same dinner for less money.
* Check out your local libraries for videos and DVDs. It's surprising what you can find in the collections, and there is usually no charge for borrowing.

Vacations

* Travel during off-peak seasons for greater savings.
* Instead of a holiday once a year, consider one every two years.
* Instead of traveling to another place, be a tourist in your own city. Visit local tourist attractions, book an appointment at a hotel spa, and eat out every day. Not only will you save on travel and accommodation costs, but you'll also really get to know your own city.
* When you do travel, stay in places where kids can stay and eat for free.
* Check out travel discounts available to American and Canadian Automobile Association (AAA & CAA) members. Members are often entitled to discounts on hotel accommodations and car rentals.

Other Silent Money Wasters

* Eliminate unnecessary insurance and upgrades on new purchases. Say no to bonuses that cost and that you are unlikely to use.

* Avoid running out of staples such as milk, bread, and coffee. They cost more to buy at the last minute at high-priced convenience stores.

* Make a point of returning unwanted or unsuitable items within the purchase return time limit. Laziness is costly to your pocketbook.

Got other money-saving ideas? Share them with the author. Contact Sylvia at <www.SylviaLim.com>.

GLOSSARY

Here's a list of definitions of some of the many words and phrases you will come across as you start to gain more knowledge about personal budgeting. Some of these words and phrases are also used throughout this book. All these terms may appear overwhelming at first, but once you understand them, they'll become second nature to you.

Amortization The repayment of a debt or loan by regular cash installments over a fixed period of time

Bankruptcy Insolvency; the legal declaration of one's inability to pay one's debts

Blue-chip stock A stock issued by a large, well-established, and reputable company that has a history of profitability and dividend payment. This type of stock is considered the least risky of all the common stocks.

Budget An estimate or projection of income and expenditures for a given period of time

Consolidation of debt A process by which a person's various loans and debts are combined into one, allowing for a

	realistic and manageable repayment plan to ultimately eliminate the liability
Consumer loan	Loans taken out primarily for the purchase of consumer goods. Consumer loans usually carry a high rate of interest.
Credit rating	A report card on a person's borrowing and repayment habits. It provides lenders with a snapshot of a potential borrower's credit-worthiness.
Dividend income	A share of the company's profit, paid out to its stockholders. Dividend income is usually distributed in the form of cash, but may on occasion be paid out in the form of stocks.
Fixed rate	An agreed rate of interest applied consistently throughout the term of a loan or investment
GIC	Guaranteed Investment Certificate; an interest-bearing loan, at a specified rate of interest, from its holder to a bank, trust company, or credit union for a term of usually one to five years
Growth stock	A common stock issued by a company that may have the potential for tremendous growth and profitability. At the same time, it also has the potential for tremendous losses. This type of stock is considered high risk among common stocks.
Junk bond	A high-yield bond that is considered a risky and speculative investment
Mortgage	A loan secured by real property
Personal financial planning	The process of mapping out short- and long-term financial strategies and implementing them to achieve one's financial objectives
Strip bond	A bond consisting of a principal certificate and an interest coupon. Dealers separate the interest coupon from the principal certificate and

sell each part separately at a discount. The coupon payments are often referred to as strips, while the principal amounts are referred to as residuals.

Term deposit   An interest-bearing loan from you to a bank, trust company, credit union, or insurance company for a fixed term at a specified rate of interest. Usually, the longer the term, the higher the rate.

Variable rate   A fluctuating rate of interest, as agreed by both lender and borrower, applied throughout the term of a loan or investment

The following Worksheets and Resources are included on the CD-ROM for use on a Windows-based PC. The documents are in MS Word and/or Excel format, as well as in PDF.

Worksheets
* Daily Spending
* Financial Goals
* Income
* Net Worth
* Revised Spending
* Weekly Spending
* Yearly Spending

Resources
* Credit Reporting Agencies
* Discount Coupons
* Personal Finance Publications
* Suggested Reading

Bonus form: Small-Business Budget

TITLES OF INTEREST IN THE SELF-COUNSEL BUSINESS SERIES

Numbers 101 for Small Business is a series of easy-to-understand guides for small-business owners, covering such topics as bookkeeping, analyzing and tracking financial information, starting a business, and growing a business. Using real-life examples, Angie Mohr teaches small-business owners how to beat the odds and turn their ideas into successful, growing companies.

Bookkeepers' Boot Camp:
Get a Grip on Accounting Basics
ISBN: 1-55180-449-2
$14.95 US/$19.95 CDN

Bookkeepers' Boot Camp teaches you how to sort through masses of information and paperwork, record what is important for your business, and grow your business for success!

* Understand your balance sheet
* Learn the basics of income statements and cash-flow statements
* Record sales cycles
* Learn how to account for inventory

Financial Management 101:
Get a Grip on Your Business Numbers
ISBN: 1-55180-448-4
$14.95 US/$19.95 CDN

Financial Management 101 is an in-depth guide on business planning. It's a kick-start course for new entrepreneurs and a wake-up call for small-business owners.

Personal Budgeting Kit

SYSTEM REQUIREMENTS

Windows:

- Windows 95, 98, ME, 2000, XP, or NT4
- Web browser Version 5 or later
- Internet connection for updates

INSTALLATION

Windows Setup:

1. Insert the CD into your CD-ROM drive. Installation should start automatically. If installation does not automatically begin, click the Start button on your desktop and choose Run.
2. In the Run dialog box, type D:\SETUP.EXE. (Replace the D with the letter for your CD-ROM drive.)
3. Click OK.
4. Follow the onscreen instructions.

AFTER INSTALLATION

IMPORTANT:

To find the MS Word and Excel versions of the forms in this kit, look for a folder that will appear on your desktop after the installation is finished.

If you have found this book useful and would like to receive a free catalog of Self-Counsel titles, please write to the appropriate address below:

Self-Counsel Press Inc.
1704 North State Street
Bellingham, WA 98225

Self-Counsel Press
1481 Charlotte Road
North Vancouver, BC V7J 1H1

Or visit us on the World Wide Web at *www.self-counsel.com*